More Praise for *Shakti Leadership*

"Gender equality, diversity, and inclusion are finally being recognized globally as good for business and for humankind. While many companies have structured programs in place to retain and grow women leaders, there is still ignorance in understanding the 'feminine' qualities that both men and women need to bring to the workplace to complement the masculine qualities that are so prevalent. As an Indian, I find that our ancient wisdom offers great value to modern business and leadership. In *Shakti Leadership*, Nilima Bhat and Raj Sisodia tap into this wisdom, as well as wisdom from other traditions, in a profound and engaging way to offer deep insights for leadership and life for men and women everywhere."

—Anand Mahindra, Chairman and Managing Director, Mahindra Group

"Nilima Bhat and Raj Sisodia put forward a compelling argument for restoring the natural balance of leadership. The importance of creating a new culture of corporate inclusiveness, where we utilize the true power of feminine qualities—such as cooperation, creativity, and empathy—cannot be underestimated in this imbalanced world. Business has a purpose beyond profits, and the argument for a new vision of leadership led by the principle of Shakti is both powerful and insightful for the sustainable future of business."

—Rakesh Sarna, Managing Director and CEO, Taj Hotels Resorts and Palaces

"*Shakti Leadership* is a timely refresher that acknowledges the weave of masculinity and femininity in our human selves. This is important in an age when we need a caring kind of capitalism, where business looks beyond the narrow objective of maximizing profits and helps people lead more fulfilling lives. We now realize that, among other things, the historically patriarchal workplace has to bring in more feminine attributes—what the authors describe as the power of Shakti. This book offers organizations and professionals many useful ideas to create a humane and resilient culture, such as drawing upon their inner reserves of strength; nurturing values such as trust, accountability, and transparency; and harmonizing male and female traits to become truly visionary leaders."

—Anu Aga, Chairperson, Teach for India, and former Chairperson, Thermax

"As Indians, we grow up soaked in our mythological wisdom. As Indian family-owned business leaders operating in a global economy, we are constantly looking to grow wings, without losing connection with our roots. Nilima and Raj offer us a model for leadership, built on many years of learning and synthesizing, that is as universal as it is dharmic, as timely as it is timeless. I strongly recommend this book to all men and women who aspire to leadership or are seeking to elevate their practice of this most essential human calling."

—Harsh Mariwala, Chairman, Marico Limited

"*Shakti Leadership* reveals the next stage of evolution and leadership in a clear, grounded, and thorough way. Nilima and Raj do a beautiful job of articulating a spectrum of complex subjects in relatable ways. They cover what are the most important wisdom-related topics that can impact leaders who want to create a world that works for all. What I loved most is that Nilima and Raj speak to difficult and important matters, such as patriarchy, without being too careful or subtle about their insights and without coming from a stance of blame or victim-hood. This is the most clear and succinct description of feminine and masculine qualities that I have seen written in a book."

—Michelle Stransky, founder of WisdomWomen

"Nilima and Raj have cocreated a book that is much needed. When we awaken to our true nature, synergize the masculine and feminine within ourselves, and discover the essence of our Shakti, we become infinitely compassionate and courageous to take responsibility for the way we live now. Leaders will find the path in this book to come together and make our organizations more conscious, leading to a peaceful, sustainable, and happier world!"

—Anil Sachdev, founder and CEO, School of Inspired Leadership

"I'm grateful to Nilima Bhat and Raj Sisodia for this insightful and timely book. Reclaiming the lost balance between masculine and feminine leadership styles is a very important part of the larger project of making the world of business more ethical—and thus more effective at creating sustainable value. It is wonderful to see the wisdom of the East being so skillfully applied to the challenges faced by modern organizations. *Shakti Leadership* is a significant contribution to the conscious capitalism movement."

—Steve McIntosh, author of *Integral Consciousness and the Future of Evolution* and President, Institute for Cultural Evolution

"This book is of vital importance! The rise of feminine power fully integrated with the healthy masculine is paramount to the development of the planet, organiza-tions, and ourselves. Nilima and Raj's outstanding work shows us, through their wisdom and clear writing, how we as leaders can harness this potential."

—Kristin Engvig, founder and CEO, WIN

"A powerful leadership model that leverages and unites our masculine and feminine energies."

—Richard Barrett, founder and Chairman, Barrett Values Centre

"*Shakti Leadership* is a bold reimagination of leadership that is both conceptually robust and immediately usable at the same time. A must-read for all those seek-ing to deeply understand the inner drives that make them the leaders they are and striving to create diverse cultures where each person can flourish."

—Shubhro Sen, Director, School of Management and Entrepreneurship, Shiv Nadar University

"*Shakti Leadership* is first about deeply understanding who we really are and why we exist and then about using that knowledge to meaningfully connect with others to cocreate a better future. It is a must-read for anyone who wants to really wake up."

—Rajeev Peshawaria, CEO, The Iclif Leadership and Governance Centre, and author of *Too Many Bosses, Too Few Leaders* and *Be the Change*

Shakti
LEADERSHIP

Shakti LEADERSHIP

Embracing Feminine and Masculine Power in Business

Nilima Bhat and Raj Sisodia

Berrett–Koehler Publishers, Inc.
a BK Business book

Berrett-Koehler Publishers, Inc.
1333 Broadway, Suite 1000, Oakland, CA 94612-1921
Tel: (510) 817-2277   Fax: (510) 817-2278   www.bkconnection.com

Ordering Information

Quantity Sales. Special discounts are available on quantity purchases by corporations, associations, and others. For details, contact the "Special Sales Department" at the Berrett-Koehler address above.

Individual Sales. Berrett-Koehler publications are available through most bookstores. They can also be ordered directly from Berrett-Koehler: Tel: (800) 929-2929; Fax: (802) 864-7626; www.bkconnection.com

Orders for College Textbook/Course Adoption Use. Please contact Berrett-Koehler: Tel: (800) 929-2929; Fax: (802) 864-7626.

Orders by U.S. Trade Bookstores and Wholesalers. Please contact Ingram Publisher Services, Tel: (800) 509-4887; Fax: (800) 838-1149; E-mail: customer.service@ingrampublisherservices.com; or visit www.ingrampublisherservices.com/Ordering for details about electronic ordering.

Berrett-Koehler and the BK logo are registered trademarks of Berrett-Koehler Publishers, Inc.

Printed in the United States of America

Berrett-Koehler books are printed on long-lasting acid-free paper. When it is available, we choose paper that has been manufactured by environmentally responsible processes. These may include using trees grown in sustainable forests, incorporating recycled paper, minimizing chlorine in bleaching, or recycling the energy produced at the paper mill.

Library of Congress Cataloging-in-Publication Data

Names: Bhat, Nilima, author. | Sisodia, Rajendra, author.
Title: Shakti leadership : embracing feminine and masculine power in business / Nilima Bhat & Raj Sisodia.
Description: First edition. | Oakland, CA : Berrett-Koehler Publishers, Inc., [2016] | Includes bibliographical references.
Identifiers: LCCN 2015049400 | ISBN 9781626564657 (pbk.)
Subjects: LCSH: Leadership. | Leadership--Religious aspects. | Shakism.
Classification: LCC HD57.7 .B494 2016 | DDC 303.3/4--dc23
LC record available at http://lccn.loc.gov/2015049400

First Edition
21 20 19 18 17 16   10 9 8 7 6 5 4 3 2 1

Interior design: Laura Lind Design   *Edit:* Lunaea Weatherstone
Cover design: Nancy Austin   *Proofread:* Henrietta Bensussen
Production service: Linda Jupiter Productions   *Index:* Paula C. Durbin-Westby

To Shakti
and everyone who helped me make the journey,

especially Ganesha, Swami Sivananda,
Sri Aurobindo and the Mother,
Daddy, Mummy, Fr. Lancy,
Vijay
Shravan and Shambhavi

—Nilima

To the extraordinary souls in the Chittasangha
("Consciousness Collaborative"),
for greatly deepening my understanding of
consciousness and leadership;

and to my mother Usha, sister Manju,
and wife Shailini,
who embody Shakti for me

—Raj

CONTENTS

FOREWORD

This remarkable new book comes at a most opportune time, an evolutionary juncture in which reinventing the possibilities of leadership can play a major positive role in all our lives. *Shakti Leadership*, based on extensive research, artfully summarizes the best of perennial wisdom, while adding powerful, real-world practices to the repertoire of leaders everywhere.

At its core, Shakti is the creative force from which all structures arise. Nilima and Raj unfold its aspects in an accessible and easily assimilated style. They guide you through powerful processes for integrating the best of Shakti Leadership into your life and organization now, such as finding presence in the midst of frenetic activity and replacing competition with partnership and dynamic balance. The book embraces the most urgent and current questions that most interest both women and men.

We particularly appreciate the interactive components of the book, which engage all aspects of being and doing to integrate the book's wisdom, chapter by chapter. With an enchanting melody of invitation and possibility, Raj and Nilima intuitively rebut the caveats and skepticism that conscious exploration can stir up. The central message really resounds throughout the book: "It's time for us to be bolder." At the heart of *Shakti Leadership*'s message is the liberation of the creative energy curtailed by thousands of years of fearing women's power, by both men and women. You are guided through inner, relational, and structural reinvention activities that both challenge and expand your creativity and your ability to step into the unknown with confidence.

Shakti Leadership is written for those willing to step out of hierarchy and into new rhythms of collaboration and invention, moving together rather than against, and welcoming intuition into the boardroom and harmony into our hearts. You experience a new understanding of presence that becomes central to unfolding a different future, and a world in which each person's creative power can flow through an integral and vital structure. In *Shakti Leadership* you'll find a series of lively dialogues that dance between logic and feeling, logos and mythos, and other dynamics that have intrigued consciousness enthusiasts for centuries. This is a book that brings many rich traditions together so that you can expand your leadership skills in core ways that will make a difference now and into the future.

Gay Hendricks and Kathlyn Hendricks
The Hendricks Institute
December 2015

A CRISIS OF CONSCIOUSNESS AND LEADERSHIP

Do we really need another book on leadership? Bookshelves the world over are groaning under the weight of a never-ending flow of leadership books. But the stark reality remains: the way we lead isn't working nearly as well as we need it to. Our current one-sided notion of a leader's power is a root cause of a host of contemporary problems, including social breakdown, environmental degradation, epidemics of stress and depression, and corruption in business and government. Men and women alike have been conditioned to value leadership qualities traditionally considered masculine: hierarchical, individualistic, and militaristic. The consequences have been dire for too long, and we can ill afford to continue to suffer them much longer. The origin of the problem is crystal clear: societies around the world have consistently and egregiously devalued qualities and perspectives traditionally deemed feminine. For all of recorded time, the wisdom and unique perspectives of over half of humanity have been largely excluded from influencing how we live and work. How can this not lead to severe dysfunction?

Seeking to reclaim feminine power and restore the long-lost balance of masculine and feminine energies for men and women alike, this book charts a new path based on timeless wisdom. Reaching into ancient spiritual and mythical teachings, we revive a feminine archetype of leadership: regenerative, cooperative, creative, and empathetic. In the Indian yogic tradition, these qualities are associated with Shakti: the source of creation, sustenance, and transformation that powers the cycle of life. We all need the primordial power and energy that is Shakti—creative, tireless, and restorative.

Leaders who understand and practice Shakti Leadership operate from a consciousness of life-giving caring, creativity, and sustainability to achieve self-mastery internally and be of selfless service to the world. When leaders of both sexes learn to embrace this mindset, we can restore sanity, elevate humanity, and heal the planet by evolving joyously and consciously together.

So Much Has Changed

We're living at a critical time. Humanity appears poised on the precipice of a great shift in our evolution. After millennia of incremental growth as a species, we appear to have reached a mutation point where our development could take a quantum leap to a whole new level in a remarkably short amount of time.

The human journey of growth and evolution certainly did not stop when we got up on our two legs, as evolutionary charts depict. In fact, we are changing and evolving at a faster rate than ever before—by orders of magnitude.

One of the factors driving these rates is the rapid aging of many societies. Driven by a combination of sharply declining birth rates and steadily increasing life expectancy, the median age has been rising in most countries around the world. In 1989, the United States reached a demographic tipping point: it was the first year that there were more adults over the age of 40 than below it. The age of 40 is a significant threshold in human life; it marks the passage into midlife and is often accompanied by a crisis of meaning and purpose. Many people come to the realization around this time in their life that the values and priorities that drove them in the past no longer feel personally relevant. They are consumed with questions such as, "What is the purpose of *my* life? What kind of legacy will I leave behind?" Many people come to the realization that life cannot be just about their own material success; there has to be more to it.

The year 1989 was also when we crossed another threshold: there were more women holding college degrees in the United States than men. Women now comprise nearly 60 percent of college enrollees and, on average, get higher grades than men. It is simply a matter of time before women dominate virtually every white-collar profession. This numerical rise of women will inevitably bring about a shift toward more feminine values in the workplace and in society at large. It will mark a fundamental shift in the world, as nothing like this has ever remotely existed before.

A little-known fact is that we human beings are rapidly becoming more analytically intelligent, as measured by IQ tests. Intelligence researcher James Flynn looked at IQ testing data going back for about 80 years. The data gets normalized to 100 every 10 years, so that the average IQ in society is always 100. Flynn looked at the raw data and found a startling pattern: humans are collectively becoming more intelligent at the rate of 3 to 4 percent every decade. Compounded over eight decades, this suggests that the average person today would have had an IQ of 131 and been in the top 2 percent of intelligence in the year 1935! This pace of change is unprecedented; we are simply not supposed to evolve at such a rapid rate. But we are.[1]

We are also on a journey of rising consciousness. The entire human journey on this planet can be seen as one of gradually waking up—both to the world around us and to our own extraordinary potential as human beings. As more of humanity has moved beyond a survival mode, we have been able to take off our blinders and see the bigger picture. Instead of just being focused on our short-term survival, we are now able to see how our actions have consequences beyond our immediate surroundings, and how we in turn are impacted by the actions of others. Once we become aware of the consequences of our actions, we also have a finer sense of what is right and what is wrong. Things that were acceptable in the past are no longer acceptable. The pace of change has been mind-boggling. Consider the following:

- 150 years ago, slavery was legal and commonplace in many countries. The United States fought a brutal civil war to end this degrading and inhuman practice, and many other countries also outlawed slavery around that time. But if you go back in human history, you find that slavery was an integral part of every major civilization. Most people, including many slaves, saw nothing wrong with it. Today, it is hard to imagine living in such a world.

- 100 years ago, hardly any women on this planet had the right to vote. In 1893, New Zealand became the first country in which all women could vote in parliamentary elections. Women attained the right to vote in the United States in 1920. In Switzerland, women did not gain the right to vote until 1971; in 2010, Switzerland swore in its first female majority government.

- 75 years ago we still had colonialism, which can be seen as another form of slavery. India was still a British colony.

- 50 years ago, there was still legally sanctioned racial segregation in many parts of the United States.

- 30 years ago, child labor, animal abuse, and environmental degradation were still common and legal in many places.

- 22 years ago, there was still apartheid in South Africa.

- Until 2004, same-sex marriage was not allowed anywhere in the United States; as of this writing, it is legal nationwide, as well as in almost 20 other countries.

Clearly, a lot has changed in a very short amount of time. As Abraham Lincoln said, "The dogmas of the quiet past are inadequate to the stormy present. As our case is new we must think anew and act anew." We are by no means done making radical changes—there is a lot more still to come. Just as the nineteenth century was about the end of slavery and the twentieth was about the end of totalitarianism, the greatest story of the twenty-first century will undoubtedly be about the end of relegating women and feminine values to second-class status.

REACHING THE BOILING POINT

When you heat water and the temperature rises, there comes a moment when the temperature can't go beyond 100 degrees centigrade, and any additional heat you put in becomes latent heat. The water gathers energy to break through the structure of its liquidity and becomes steam. There's a quantum change from what it was to what it is now. It takes time to reach that point, but when it comes, change happens quickly.

Humanity appears to be at that point today; we're on the cusp. Many people in diverse fields are sensing that we are at a singular moment of discontinuity. Things are poised to change in fundamental ways; we're either going to boil over and evolve or we're going to crash and self-destruct.

The "fire-under-our-@$$" is Shakti, the power of Nature's evolution itself.

The Mother was the spiritual collaborator of Sri Aurobindo, the famed twentieth-century Indian mystic. She said, "The only hope for the future is in a change of man's consciousness and the change is bound to come. But it is left to men to decide if they will collaborate for this change or if it will have to be enforced upon them by the power of crashing circumstances. So, wake up and collaborate!"[2]

We are at a very important time of great change, a latent state of tremendous tension. This is being seen in our personal as well as work lives, and in what's happening with the environment, and within our social structures. We think the chaos is only in our lives, but it's everywhere, so don't take it personally! To quote from Martin Luther King Jr.'s famous "I Have a Dream" speech, there is "a fierce urgency of now."[3] Our crisis is a crisis of consciousness. As the expression goes, a problem cannot be solved at the level of consciousness at which it was created. We have to mobilize the forces that will evolve us to a new level.

Our crisis of consciousness is also a crisis of leadership, because ultimately it is leaders who must solve problems. They must take the initiative instead of being victims of the situation. Leaders of the old consciousness caused the problems we face today; leaders with new consciousness are needed to solve them. Most current business and leadership models are clearly inadequate; the evidence of dysfunction is everywhere. In the workplace, employee engagement levels are shockingly low around the world. In the United States, on average, only three out of ten employees are engaged in their work, five are indifferent, and two are actively hostile.[4] Appallingly, these are some of the highest numbers globally; worldwide, Gallup estimates that employee engagement is only 13 percent. Seven out of eight employees feel that they work for companies that do not care about them as human beings. Such unhappy employees cannot help but go home and infect their spouses and children with that unhappiness and frustration. Health care costs are soaring largely because of an epidemic of chronic illness. Most chronic illness is caused by stress, and most stress is caused by work—it's a vicious cycle.

It doesn't have to be this way. Work does not have to deplete us; in fact, it can be one of the most meaningful things in our lives. But to get there, we have to recognize that our workplaces have largely been devoid of a crucial part of what it means to be human: the feminine aspect.

SHAKTI: THE POWER BASE FOR
CONSCIOUS CAPITALISM

Recent years have brought a dawning realization that we need to rethink the foundational bases of capitalism, starting with the idea that it is solely rooted in the pursuit of narrowly construed and material self-interest. Human beings have multiple primal drives, including the need to survive and the need to care. Love and work define what it means to be human. The emerging Conscious Capitalism philosophy is about blending the two. It starts with asking the question "What is the purpose of business?" The answer: it is *not* to maximize profits but rather to uplift humanity, by meeting real needs, providing meaningful work, spreading prosperity, and enabling more of us to lead more fulfilling and more fully human lives. The second pillar is stakeholder integration. Companies should consciously create multifaceted value for customers, employees, communities, suppliers, investors, the environment, and beyond. The well-being of each stakeholder should be seen as an end in itself, not as a means to the end of making more money for shareholders.

The next pillar of Conscious Capitalism is that companies should create nurturing and life-enhancing cultures imbued with values such as trust, accountability, caring for, and transparency. Most businesses are characterized by high levels of fear and stress; conscious businesses are built on love and care.

Perhaps the most fundamental pillar of Conscious Capitalism is about reimagining leadership. Conscious leaders are fundamentally selfless. They care about people and the purpose of the enterprise ahead of their own ego or personal enrichment. They seek power *with* rather than power *over* people.

The stated purpose of Conscious Capitalism is to "elevate humanity" through the practice of business as a force for good. Its narrative is centered on the need to cultivate a new consciousness of how to lead and conduct business. For that, we are going to need a new base of power. "Business as usual" runs on ego-based power; Conscious Capitalism runs on Shakti-based power. Shakti is power that comes from an infinite source within you that you can tap into at all times. This power is linked to everything, including money, which is what business has traditionally focused on.

Why do we consider Shakti an infinite source? Unlike the ego, which can be broken down, no one can take Shakti-based power away from you. You may feel that your power derives from your position. If you are the CEO today, you are vested with privilege and power, but if you are not CEO tomorrow, who would you be? Would people still respect you, look up to you, follow you? Can you hold your sense of self, and can you help bring about meaningful outcomes from that true source rather than from the position vested in you?

This whole game is about power; everyone wants and needs power. Without power, everything remains stagnant. Nothing can become manifest, become actualized. Shakti is the transformative power that manifests ideas into reality.

You may ask, why Shakti? Why not, for example, the Tao, which works with the core principle of *qi* (pronounced *chi*), not just as a philosophy but also its power? The compelling difference in the yogic tradition is that Shakti is not an impersonal, inanimate force; it is intelligent and conscious. You can enter into relationship with it. Once you do, it serves you, moves you, and fuels you.

Critically, Shakti also brings in the feminine dimension, which is lacking in the world and has been for a long time—if not for all time. Shakti is understood as creative and generative, and is therefore represented as feminine. Men as well as women can tap into it. In the yogic tradition, the human journey is one that seeks to end the duality between masculine and feminine, or Shiva and Shakti. It's not about "separate but equal," but about evolving into an integrated and synergistic combination of both.

How does Shakti fuel us? Consider the north and south poles of a horseshoe magnet. There is potential in the space between the poles, but you can only tap into that energy when you insert a wire in that space. We exist in this duality and polarity between male and female. We may prefer our traditionally masculine or traditionally feminine leadership styles, but that means we're basically split beings, operating from half of our selves. As a result, we barely operate, because energy only flows when both polarities are leveraged.

Shakti, the power that is latent in your being, gets unlocked when you become whole, flexible, and aligned with your unique purpose. Shakti is an evolutionary force, moving you toward fulfillment. The more you put yourself in accord with your purpose as a being and as a leader, the more energy starts rising up in you to move you forward. There is a beautiful reinforcing pattern there: the more you are on purpose, the more power you get to meet your purpose. It is similar to the idea of being "in flow."[5]

Becoming a conscious leader requires a transformational journey. You do not become a conscious leader just by getting behavioral skill training in "what leaders do." Deeper, foundational shifts are required to connect you to new and true bases of consciousness and power. The person you are is the leader you are; therefore, you have to make the journey inward to transform yourself. The "hero's journey," Joseph Campbell's masterwork, maps perfectly onto modern leadership and business. You need to push beyond your known zone. It takes hard work and you will face many obstacles along the way. It is also a dangerous journey in which you're going to have to "die" in some ways.

Human beings and the universe are evolving in a certain direction; there is a distinct trajectory that can be discerned. There is an evident purpose to this process; it is not all based on random mutations. If we can flow into that trajectory and be part of it, rather than be at cross-purposes with it, we can have access to extraordinary power. We become agents of what needs to be. If not, these infinitely powerful forces quickly cancel out our feeble efforts. How do you connect with a place that fuels you continuously? How do you become a whole person in order to be a whole leader? How do you become a flexible person in order to be a flexible leader? These are the questions this book will answer.

REINVENTING LEADERSHIP

Leadership is a perennial subject of analysis and discussion. While much has been achieved in transforming concepts of leadership into powerful tools for business and other societal institutions, there continues to be a need for leadership to evolve in more holistic ways. In particular, there is a need for a leadership paradigm that taps into the best aspects of the higher masculine and feminine natures that lie dormant in men and women alike.

However, women and men who are sensing and awakening to this need don't always know where to find guidance and support. That is the gap we seek to address.

The prevailing leadership paradigm, born of the patriarchy and rooted in militaristic thinking, drastically overemphasizes certain masculine values. It is primarily an *outside-in, competency-based* approach. It is still predominantly based on hierarchy, command-and-control, and using "carrots and sticks" to induce desired behaviors. This book aims to restore balance and wholeness in leaders by awakening them to powerful, innately feminine leadership capacities that lie dormant within them. We do so through an *inside-out, consciousness-based* approach that sources directly from Shakti, the primordial power and intelligence that creates, sustains, and evolves our world. Since it is the original, creative source, which bears Life, it is considered feminine. It complements the principle of awareness or consciousness, which is considered masculine (see sidebar).

A Quick Primer on Shakti

In the yogic tradition, Shakti is the female principle of divine energy. It is understood as power—even as absolute power. Shakti enables the awakening of consciousness. It is seen as a feminine energy because it is responsible for creation, just as mothers are responsible for giving birth. Shakti manifests as energy, power, movement, change, and nature. It is the maternal principle, symbolizing nourishment, warmth, and security. The world knows no greater love than the love of a mother, who offers her body to carry and nourish the child and sacrifices herself to raise the child. The paternal principle is Shiva, symbolizing pure consciousness. Shiva is seen as the "unchanging, unlimited, and unswayable observer."[6]

Yogic philosophy refers to three forms of Shakti impacting the body, mind, and spirit:

- *Prana Shakti* is the life force of the physical body, which governs our actions, organs, and functions.

- *Chitta Shakti* is governance of our mental functions, such as intelligence, thinking, emotions, memory, desires, decision-making, planning, and so on.

- *Atma Shakti* is the "causal and creative power of consciousness."[7]

At the advent of creation, our beings became split into this Shiva-Shakti duality. Each of us carries Shiva and Shakti within us as the masculine and feminine principles. We carry within us a powerful force that is striving to reunite with our complementary parts. The dissolving of this duality is the aim of yoga, a word that translates to "coming together."

It is only when Shiva and Shakti come together that there can be any meaningful action, movement, and creation. Energy that is not informed by consciousness is disordered and chaotic. Consciousness without energy is dormant and cannot cause anything to happen.

This idea is not limited to the yogic tradition. The Gnostic mystic Simon the Magus is believed to have said, "The universal eons consist of two branches, without beginning or end, which spring from one root . . . the invisible power and the unknowable silence. One of these branches is manifested from above and is the universal consciousness ordering all things and is designated male. The other branch is female and is the producer of all things."[8]

Most leadership books focus on what leaders do, and some on how they do it. As Joseph Jaworski, author of the landmark books *Synchronicity: The Inner Path of Leadership* and *Source: The Inner Path of Knowledge Creation*, puts it, the key question is "from where?" From where do great leaders draw the power and wisdom to lead as well as they do? That source is Shakti. It is the source of authentic, effective, life-affirming leadership that combines the mature masculine with the mature feminine into a life-enhancing whole. Shakti Leadership is about a new way for men and women to lead and live. By coming into our full presence and aligning with the natural forces of evolution, we can tap into limitless power in pursuit of noble goals.

We believe that all leaders today—men and women—need to become whole by integrating their masculine and feminine natures. All leaders need to come into their true power and unleash their creativity and inclusive-growth abilities to help resolve the multiple crises we face on many fronts: economic, social, cultural, political, and environmental.

Many women continue to approach leadership as "men in women's clothing," with predictably unhappy results for themselves and for the organizations they lead. Most men, equally tragically, remain disconnected from a vital aspect of their humanness—their innate feminine qualities.

A new consciousness of the feminine is urgently needed. Most men and women, socialized by the patriarchy, have overdeveloped their masculine selves and focused on achieving tasks. The time has now come for *both* men and women to awaken to the nurturing, relational, and inclusive feminine within.

This book is about leadership as it should be for everybody. It is about thinking about power in a different way. Power is the source of corruption and exploitation when it is purely ego-based, when it is not in harmony with where evolution is taking us. When we become aligned with evolutionary forces, we do not need to grasp for power and use it as an instrument of manipulation, oppression, and suppression, serving our own ego and nothing else.

Shakti Leadership is based on authentic, true power. It leads to personal fulfillment and a positive impact on the lives of others.

More than focusing on leading others, this book is first about leading yourself as a conscious capitalist or aspiring change agent. It is a comprehensive primer on how to "be the change" you want to see in your business. It is a step-by-step guide to how you can live a fuller, less conflicted, less fragmented, and more harmonious life. The book tells you what to expect on the journey you are going to have to undertake to get there.

It is also about recognizing the larger context in which you make this heroic journey. We live in a time of uncovering the magnificent commonalities and equally priceless complementarities between men and women. It is not about "the end of men and the rise of women," the misleading title of Hanna Rosin's important book. Rather, it is about an extraordinary union that has been many millennia in the making, toward which evolution has been pointing. It is not about a dissolution of gender identities but instead a celebration of the glorious symphony of harmonies that results when complementary forces finally start to act in concert and thus fulfill their infinite potential. It is about humanity progressing to the next stage of our evolution, one in which men and women alike operate from a place of authentic power—power exercised *with* each other rather than over each other. It is time to end the battle of the sexes and recognize that we are far more than our individual genders. It is time to become fully human.

One

SEEKING SHAKTI

*When soul-force awakens, it becomes irresistible
and conquers the world. This power is inherent in
every human being.*

—Mahatma Gandhi

WHAT IS SHAKTI?

India's ancient adepts intuited and experienced the existence of
a source of infinite creative power and loving intelligence. This
same power and intelligence has created everything around us
and within us. It is what enables our fingernails to grow and our
minds to contemplate the deepest mysteries of the universe. They
called that source Shakti: the generative, fiercely loving power
that fuels all creation and animates consciousness. All of reality is
intelligent; it is conscious. It is evolved by its own innate power —
which creates, preserves, and transforms itself endlessly.

Think of an exquisite car that's been designed and built to
perfection. Without the right fuel, the car is useless. Similarly,
consciousness by itself is sterile, still, and inert. Shiva — the embodiment of consciousness in yogic traditions — is *shava* (corpse)
without Shakti. Shakti is the power that fuels everything.

Shiva represents consciousness and Shakti represents energy. Each one needs the other. Shakti needs Shiva to ground it, otherwise it becomes chaotic; Shiva without Shakti is inert and sterile.

Shakti is understood as supremely intelligent and infinitely varied; it represents the full spectrum of energies that make up the universe. It is the fueling, dynamic power, the primordial cosmic energy that manifests this world and sustains it, from the smallest subatomic spaces to the whole cosmos. As author and spiritual teacher Sally Kempton puts it, "Shakti is the quality in life that gives life its luscious nature, its juiciness, its movement, its energy, its dynamism, love, joy, blissfulness, meaningfulness. Shakti runs our life, giving the energy that makes our heart beat and our brain have thoughts."[1]

We all have available to us this infinitely powerful and intelligent source to draw upon, yet most of us try to manufacture our own meager and distorted power—or we try and extract it from others. We rely on our own egos and worldly position or other manmade constructs—constructs that we have invested with value and power but that are ultimately devoid of significance.

Advanced degrees and the trappings of success notwithstanding, if we are not rooted in our own creative power—our personal Shakti—we are merely a shell without a soul, a car without fuel; a being without its animating principle. We cannot come into any level of mastery until we become aware of and access this true power. But it must be responsibly exercised, nourished, and expressed for the fulfillment of life, rather than to serve a narrow self-interest.

True Power versus False Power

In her thought-provoking book *The Soul of Money*, Lynne Twist shares the three toxic myths of scarcity that many have come to accept as truths about money globally: that there's not enough, that more is better, and "that's just the way it is."[2] Money is just one embodiment of power or energy; these myths can be applied to all expressions of power.

Reflecting our uneasy relationship with the very idea, the literature on power is marked by deep and seemingly intractable disagreements over how it should be understood. Leadership is the purposeful exercise of power to achieve desired outcomes. It involves applying one's will and life force to generate results. Unfortunately, most leaders throughout history have played fear-based or force-based power games. But that kind of power requires someone to lose in order for someone else to win. As Sally Kempton says, "Ego-based power comes from the experience of your own limitation and lack. You feel that because you are separate from the source, your power is limited to what you can grasp, stand for, hold. That is essentially a weak position because your sources are finite and therefore you're very concerned with holding onto that power, and you're threatened by anyone else who seems to have power."[3]

What, then, is the difference between true power and false power? True power is not power *over*, but power *with*. It's the difference between competing against colleagues for personal gain versus leveraging everyone's capabilities and strengths toward common ends. When true power is exercised, no one has to lose for someone else to win.

Shakti Leaders Speak: On True Power

Caryl Stern, CEO of U.S. Fund for UNICEF, defines power as the opportunity and ability to have an impact:

I think for a really long time power was defined as money. For me, power is about the ability to bring about change and have impact. When I think about where am I powerful, what have I done in the world—I have helped to raise a lot of money, that's great. But I have also changed how people feel about coming to work; that's really powerful to me. I have helped my children to see that the world is bigger than themselves; that's really powerful to me. I really think that's the definition of power—being able to impact others.[4]

In our world, in our lives, and in leadership, people frequently engage in ego- and fear-based power games. Such power transactions always result in win-lose dualities. They are based on the presumption that there isn't enough power to go around, that you need to extract power or steal it from those around you.

We will show you how to shift from dealing in the power of privilege—a win-lose proposition based on a power source that you can lose—to drawing from your innate, infinite power source, Shakti, which no one can take away from you. We need a radical shift from the way in which power has been gained and for the most part abused in the past, to a whole new base from which to operate: the power of presence. Unless we plug into presence and connect to the source of our true Shakti, we will continue to operate on false power.

Women especially need to learn how to operate with true power. Women who are not in touch with their wholeness and their Shakti are reduced to fighting for the scraps left over by men. One recurring theme that comes in interviews with genuinely puzzled male CEOs is, "Help me understand why I see women, more than men, work against women. Not only do they not look out for each other, but they often actively manipulate and scheme to keep each other down. That kind of behavior leads me to think women are their own worst enemies." This arises because most women are not plugged into true power; instead, they're working on a little corner of the field while the men, in the gender-based privilege of which they are largely unaware, are playing the big field. In this little corner, it is women versus women. The patriarchy has socialized and conditioned women into this to such an extent that most women don't even realize it.

Lasting positive outcomes can only come from the exercise of true power. Even if we think we are getting somewhere with our ego-based efforts, they disintegrate and do not endure. It is a waste of our time and energy.

Furthermore, tapped into their own unlimited source, Shakti-based leaders are able to share power with others and encourage them to get in touch with their own power. Presence is positively contagious; simply by modeling your Shakti-based power, you give others permission and inspiration to access their own. Some honest reflection will reveal that any lasting positive outcomes you have ever had, have come from exercising Shakti (the force for greater good) rather than privilege (the force of self-interest).

Shakti is the abundant, unlimited fuel, the power of life that makes electrons move and galaxies grow and seeds sprout and trees flower. By learning to tap into that unlimited source, you can have power *with* others, rather than power *over* them.

Reflections

- Think of a key relationship in your life. How do you exercise power in this relationship? Is it mostly power over or power with?

- Think of a person who models "power-over" leadership and someone who models "power-with" leadership. What can you learn about your own relationship with power?

- How can you watch for "power-over" dynamics and shift to "power-with" dynamics from now on?

- Notice how and when you may be giving away your power or unconsciously tend to lose it. Why do you think this happens? How can you prevent it?

THE FEMININE PRINCIPLE

Shakti is seen as inherently feminine and is personified in the yogic tradition in various goddesses. As the source of all things, Shakti is personified and referred to as "the Divine Mother," who worshippers and yoga practitioners experience as a being and with whom they enter into dialogue and a conscious relationship.

All over the world, societies, cultures, religions, philosophies, art forms, and literature make reference to and draw upon feminine energy personified in the Mother Goddess. Much of physical existence is given a feminine identity, such as when we refer to Mother Nature or Mother Earth. Yet for virtually all of recorded history, the feminine has been controlled and subjugated by the masculine, which deep down secretly fears the Mother's unfathomable depth and creative power.

The essential sustaining qualities of the feminine principle are present in our personal lives as the nurturing love and support shared with loved ones. However, it is largely absent from our professional lives. "Business as usual" has overvalued traditionally masculine qualities, while denying and undervaluing feminine capacities. The prevailing business culture is hypermasculine and holds most feminine qualities in contempt. To become balanced and integrated, organizations of all kinds need to value and cultivate feminine energies and qualities within their cultures—on the part of both men and women.

Shakti Leaders Speak: On Feminine Energy

Casey Sheahan, former CEO of Patagonia, recalls:

At Patagonia, the workforce is 55 percent female and 45 percent male. The energy within all organizations falls into two basic places. The first is what I call male ambitious energy, the second, which I think is ultimately a more powerful force, is female creative energy. The first energy is a frictional energy, while the second is a more conscious energy that is inspired by passion and higher purpose. You know when you're in that place because the mind is intelligent and clear; it knows what the problem to be solved is and it can see its way toward solutions that work for all the stakeholders who might be affected. The other side, male/masculine ambitious energy, is characterized by greed, power, self-centricity, ego, fear, insecurity, and anger.... This frictional energy is what caused the problems in the global economic crisis. You saw it play out on Wall Street in the last twenty years and in many of the failed corporations that were actually cheating their shareholders and the government. They were businesses that had no underlying purpose other than to bring in money. The drive of that energy is all about the individuals: their image, their status. These individuals lack connection and vision, and are incomplete as human beings. They lack something inside that prevents them from being complete, and their companies from being complete. Such businesses and organizations frequently engage in wrong actions instead of right actions.[5]

STEPPING INTO FEMININE POWER

What we see in society today reflects the omnipresent impact of a hypermasculine culture. Author and cultural theorist Jean Kilbourne has been observing and documenting the pervasive and perverse impact the culture of exploitation and objectification has had on both men and women. She observes:

> Some young women act more macho and crude in order to be more powerful. That has a lot to do with this culture's definition of power, and that power is defined as being one-up—power over somebody else rather than power being one's own ability to be effective and to make change. If that's the definition of power that girls get—and it is—and if that's what they see being rewarded, it's not surprising that they try that on themselves. Feminine values get lip service but very little respect; in fact there's a lot of contempt for them. So that's a very powerful message that girls are getting, about how they can be powerful. The only definition right now in this culture is to be more like a man.[6]

Miss Representation, a film by Jennifer Siebel Newsom, depicts how media portrayals and the objectification of women rob women of political power, making them less likely to want to be political leaders. It also makes it difficult for the women who do try. Jean Kilbourne comments, "A female political candidate has to project femininity—because otherwise she is savaged—and she also has to project strength. And if you've got a situation where strength is seen as unfeminine, it puts her in an impossible double bind. If she's strong, she's not feminine; if she's feminine, she's weak. Girls see this all around them."[7]

How can women reclaim their power after being so harshly objectified for so long? Jean Kilbourne does see some cause for optimism: "I think more and more people are beginning to see that these stereotypes and definitions of power aren't getting us anywhere; in fact, they're causing a lot of harm. What it's going to take is a critical mass of people who say we've got to change this, because it is doing serious harm to us and to our children."[8]

The fact is that women already have a great deal of power in the world, but they don't always recognize it. If they can step into the power they already have, they can bring about rapid and wide-ranging global change.

Twenty years ago, there was only one female CEO running a Fortune 500 company; there are now twenty-two. While it is still a very low percentage, the trajectory is encouraging. There used to be only a small handful of women in the US Senate at any one time; now there are twenty. The progress is steady, but still far too slow. *Miss Representation* points out that if these changes continue at their current rate it will take something like five hundred years to finally achieve equality in Congress! Something must happen to bring about change more quickly. As Jean Kilbourne puts it, "There's all this power out there, but it hasn't been grasped or been utilized."[9]

BLENDING POSITIVE FEMININE AND MASCULINE CAPACITIES

Within each of us, there is a feminine element that is both distinct from and entwined with a masculine element. There is a purpose for this: to generate the creative tension within and from which evolution can move toward its own fulfillment. We need to leverage this internal diversity in a way that allows each individual to find a unique balance of expression freely for themselves.

Traditionally feminine capacities that are gifts of tapping into Shakti include qualities such as surrender, receptivity, adaptability, intuition, creativity, beauty, flow, sensuality, nurturing, affection, sharing, gentleness, patience, vulnerability, empathy, inclusion, openness, variety/flavor, trust, and harmony.[10] But when taken too far, feminine qualities can manifest in undesirable ways, such as smothering, being seen as overly sentimental, needy, dependent, exploited, unfocused, irrational, weak, and manipulative. These are considered hyperfeminine or immature feminine qualities.

Likewise, positive masculine capacities include freedom, direction, logic, reason, focus, integrity, structure, stability, passion, independence, discipline, confidence, awareness, discernment, authenticity, strength, clarity, assertiveness, order, and convergence.[11] Hyper- or immature masculine qualities manifest as aggressive, cruel, mechanical, arrogant, insensitive, violent, power-hungry, and spiritually empty.

Of course, to categorize certain characteristics as traditionally masculine or feminine is not to say any of them are innate to men or women. Sally Kempton points to the danger of pigeonholing men and women based on gender:

> I have a bit of a problem with the idea that the feminine is naturally nurturing and emotional and the masculine is naturally competitive and aggressive. I actually think that both genders are nurturing in their own way and aggressive in their own way. I would say that, in an individual, Shakti is really much more about finding your personal source of the vibrant fountain of power which is moving through your unique configuration — which applies to men and women.[12]

Even as women rightfully fight for equal rights, opportunity, and status, it does not take away from the need to maintain this primary polarity in a healthy balance.

Shakti Leaders Speak: On Masculine and Feminine Qualities

Former president of Southwest Airlines Colleen Barrett recalls:

I've learned most of my lessons the hard way, because I've made mistakes. When you make them and you realize it, you're fine as long as you don't make the same mistake twice. I've learned the value of discipline; that's a masculine trait. I've also learned that even if you have to make tough decisions based on what is best for your organization as a whole, you can still keep your friendships. For example, you can terminate someone because it was the right thing to do for the company, but you can still keep your friendship with that person as long as you handle it in a positive way. I think lots of people struggle with that, male or female. Of course, your heart aches. If you ever feel good about terminating somebody, then there's something wrong with you as a leader to begin with. But I have kept close friendships with many, many people that I had to let go for one reason or another. [13]

Author and educator Judy Sorum Brown notes that "leadership is . . . holding both sides and valuing both."[14] John Gerzema and Michael D'Antonio's research for the book *The Athena Doctrine* also supports the idea that individuals recognize the value of both types of traits. Eighty-one percent of survey respondents agreed that "(whether) man or woman, you need both masculine and feminine traits to thrive in today's world." Gerzema and D'Antonio note that individuals who "include feminine strategies in their decision making are twice as optimistic about their future."[15]

A truly conscious leader is able to call on positive masculine and feminine qualities regardless of what gender they are. They know when it is beneficial to use more masculine or feminine energy, and are sensitive to the negative aspects of each. But most leaders disown their innate feminine capacities, which are devalued, and always choose more masculine capacities because these are what are seemingly rewarded.

Transitioning from Old to New

Human history is one long litany of the consequences of masculine values such as conquest and domination. Many increasingly recognize that the future needs to be more feminine, rooted in nurturing and caring. How will we get there? Will it take a revolution? Author and social activist extraordinaire Lynne Twist has a beautiful way to describe the transformation process: the simultaneous "hospicing" of what needs to pass on and the "midwifing" of the new wholeness:

> In the Pachamama Alliance, we call ourselves "pro-activists," which means we're standing for, not against. I'm standing for a vision and I know there are things in the way blocking that vision. There are structures and belief systems that have become rigid and calcified, causing people to behave in ways that are inconsistent with their humanity. They are not bad people. When we can look from the depth of our humanity and the humanity of others, we see that we're all caught in some sort of a weird trance. If you can wake up from it, what's waiting for you is love, compassion, forgiveness, commitment, courage and authenticity—true power, but it's blocked by the old way of doing things. We need to hospice the death of these old structures and systems that no longer serve us. We don't need to kill them; they're not viable or sustainable so they're dying a natural death anyway. If we hospice their natural death they will die more quickly and with some respect and some grace, because they were useful until they became obsolete. We need to hospice the death of those structures and systems while we midwife the birth of the new structures and systems that are so obvious to us now. Midwifing and hospicing are acts of love and witness. A midwife doesn't give birth; a midwife witnesses and allows natural birth to take place. A hospice worker doesn't destroy or kill; a hospice worker witnesses and allows something to die gracefully with dignity. In many ways, that's the great work of our time, as Thomas Berry says: to transform the human presence from one that is destructive to a mutually enhancing and

nurturing presence on this planet. It's an act of love, to wake up
from the trance we've been caught in and re-dream the world
from a place that's more conscious, more highly evolved, more
loving. Rather than a "you *or* me" paradigm, it's a "you *and* me"
paradigm, where you don't have to make it at my expense and
I don't have to make it at your expense. Instead, you and I can
both make it at no one's expense and everyone's benefit.[16]

To enact those two great duties of our time requires us to cultivate presence (a deep connection to our higher/universal self)
and tap into its power (Shakti) to fuel the process. Indeed, in the
idea of lovingly hospicing the old and midwifing the new, Lynne is
describing the ongoing work of Shakti, the evolutionary process
of the universe itself that we are called to flow with and manifest
as leaders.

Of course, this is easier said than done. Humanity is poised on
its greatest evolutionary adventure yet, but our survival depends
on our success at making this transition. Are we up to the challenge? How can we learn to source from the ground of power that
is Shakti? How can we embody it and manifest from it?

THE HEROIC JOURNEY

Finding our Shakti and coming into our own power requires us to
be tested: for our capacity to bear it and our worthiness to wield
it. The stages of the awakening of Shakti are best described as a
"heroic journey."

The concept of the hero's journey, or the monomyth of man, is
the enduring legacy of Joseph Campbell, one of the most profound
thinkers of recent times. An anthropologist by training, Campbell
studied the mythologies of cultures around the world. Eventually,
he discovered what was common to all mythologies. From his
study and understanding came his book *The Hero with a Thousand
Faces*. His work is easily recognized in many Hollywood movies
because they follow the arc that he uncovered of the mythic or
heroic journey. The *Star Wars* series is one well-known example.

The hero's journey is about coming of age, moving from innocence to maturity and individuation. It is about the process of coming into our own power and becoming the person we are meant to be—not the person we were conditioned to be by a parent, spouse, or sibling.[17]

We are each the heroes and heroines of our own life story. The heroic journey is a universal one that transcends history, geography, and culture. What we learn through the journey that we think is deeply personal to us is actually completely universal. It applies equally to our personal and professional lives, because in truth there is no difference between them; the person you are is the leader you are.

The journey is archetypal, meaning it displays a powerful "set pattern" that seems to be driving individuals and their experience. Though our journeys may seem very different on the surface, they're actually playing out universal patterns. There are recognizable stages and characters common to all journeys, which we will look at more closely later in the book (Figure 1.1).

Figure 1.1—*Stages of the Heroic Journey*

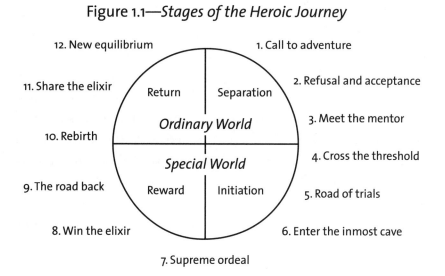

Adapted from *The Writer's Journey, Christopher Vogler.*

The heroic journey is about fulfilling one's higher purpose. It requires extraordinary effort and demands that we develop many new capacities. It is called a heroic journey because coming into our own and maturing into all that we can be takes great courage. When we journey, we cannot remain the person we were; we will arrive at journey's end as a more potent and consequential being.

The journey begins, as it must, in the ordinary world. At some point, a separation is forced upon the hero, in response to a "call to adventure." The hero initially refuses to heed the call; after all, it's usually more comfortable for a person to stay where he or she is. If you're Frodo, you want to stay in the Shire! The hero refuses the call until forced to accept it by some set of circumstances. As Elizabeth Appell put it, "The day came when the risk to remain tight in a bud was more painful than the risk it took to blossom." Each person has to find the willpower or passion inside themselves to accept the challenge.

When the moment to embark on the journey comes, an ally force shows up just in time: the hero meets the mentor (Gandalf in *The Lord of the Rings*, Dumbledore for *Harry Potter*). The mentor helps the hero cross the threshold from the ordinary world into a whole new world—the magical or the special world. The hero undergoes a slew of trials before entering the innermost cave, where he must confront a supreme ordeal. On the other side, after he overcomes the ordeal, there awaits some kind of an unexpected reward, which Campbell calls "the elixir." From there, the hero has to find his way back. There's a rebirth in the return to the ordinary world, to the place where he started. His journey is complete only when he shares the elixir with the world that he left and has now returned to. He finds a new equilibrium and is deeply transformed from the person he was when he left.

Our colleague and fellow traveler Vijay Bhat has cogently summarized the heroic journey, originally from Campbell's work and incorporating other sources such as Joseph Jaworski.[18] We share his synthesis here with his permission:

It begins in a familiar setting that appears idyllic and comforting on the surface but is actually a "wasteland," where old concepts, ideals, and emotional patterns no longer fit and where we may be living an inauthentic life.

Change is imminent. The call to adventure comes in many ways, both subtle and explicit. We are asked to give ourselves to something larger, to become what we were meant to be.

Some who are called choose to go. Others wrestle with denial and anxiety until they can overcome their fear. We refuse the call because we are insecure about risking what we have, because we dread being separated or ostracized, and because we sense danger—we might die.

Deep down, we sense that yielding to the design of the universe and cooperating with destiny will bring great personal power and responsibility. Yet we still don't feel ready.

As if from nowhere appears the guiding light: someone or something that shows the way, equips us and pushes us over the threshold to an unfamiliar, magical world that awaits.

We pass beyond the borders of the known into the void, a domain without maps, a place of both terror and opportunity. The perilous journey begins and we face a series of tests and trials, placed before us by fierce enemies whom we must overcome or circumvent.

If we have truly and fully committed ourselves to the journey, we are supported by invisible hands—powerful forces in the form of allies who speed us along and nurture our growth and preparedness.

On this road of trials, our commitment is frequently challenged, and we have many occasions to enjoy success and to learn from failure. Crossing many barriers, we endure the agony of rising beyond our personal limitations and growing spiritually.

Inevitably, we face a supreme ordeal, where we alone must confront our greatest fear and weakness—our shadow. It is our ultimate "break down or break through" point. If we succeed in transcending our shadow, it yields us the elixir we seek. In the process, we die to the old and emerge fundamentally transformed.

It is not easy to leave behind the bliss and thrill of the magical world and return to the almost forgotten place from which we came. But with the quest accomplished, we triumphantly carry back the elixir to restore and rejuvenate society.

Upon returning, it can be difficult to absorb the counter-blows of reasonable queries, hard resentments, and good people at a loss to comprehend the drama that has unfolded. But by now, we have become a potent new being, capable of handling these shocks and prepared to journey forth, again and again, in service of the community.

We are each the heroes of our own lives. Many of us have already journeyed and overcome profound challenges and ordeals. Know that you can journey again; you have the capacity and the power and the courage. You can overcome obstacles and your fear. If you didn't answer the call to adventure in the past, forgive yourself. Perhaps you were scared, thought you couldn't do it, or listened to other people and went against your own instincts. Take a deep breath and realize that this, too, is a part of being the hero.

Exercise

This exercise is about getting in touch with experiences that you may not have thought much about. Events happen and you compartmentalize them without much examination because life pushes you inexorably forward: there is always the next project or the next deadline to meet in your personal or professional life. In this way, significant episodes in your life are left unprocessed, unacknowledged, and unhonored. It is important in the journey of life to stop and remember those important times where something significant occurred. It's important to stop and feel gratitude and recognize that what you have accomplished is no small thing.

Think back to an ordeal you successfully overcame and its core stages. Ask yourself:

- What was the crisis? How were you shaken out of your comfort zone?

- Did you heed the call or refuse/resist it? Why?

- How were you tested? Who were your allies and enemies?

- What was your greatest fear? How did you overcome it?

- What new capacities did you gain? How did you mature from the experience?

- How have you shown up differently as a person since then? As a leader?

- What are you offering the world, and how has it changed for the better?

You may realize that you never framed your success stories in terms of the heroic journey. People go through many journeys but fail to recognize the transformational process they underwent. There is great value in making this conscious; once we understand how the journey tends to unfold, we can journey again and again with less fear and greater ease and effectiveness.

The calling and capacity to embark on the hero's journey are in all of us. Many now teach from Joseph Campbell's *The Hero with a Thousand Faces*, inspiring people to realize that they can be heroes instead of continuing as ordinary beings or far worse as victims.

Becoming a Shakti Leader requires undertaking a heroic journey. We will revisit this idea throughout the book. In this chapter, we talked a bit about what Shakti is, the need for finding a true balance between feminine and masculine capacities, and the difference between false power and true power. In the next chapter, we'll introduce the framework for Shakti Leadership, an original synthesis born out of our inner work and our work with entrepreneurs, consciousness practitioners, and business leaders.

2

LEADING WITH SHAKTI

*Only three things happen naturally in organizations:
friction, confusion, and underperformance.
Everything else requires leadership.*

—Peter Drucker

For life to generate and flourish, you need both the seed and the soil. Put the best possible seed into toxic or depleted soil and it will not grow. On the other hand, even with the most fertile, nurturing soil, a damaged or flawed seed will not develop into anything of lasting value or impact. Both seed and soil need to be addressed to bring about positive transformation in the world. This book is about helping you develop yourself, as the seed, and also as a leader who has the capacity to improve the quality of the soil—the context in which you lead—over time.

Shakti Leadership is a powerful and practical leadership model that consciously leverages masculine and feminine energies to heal, restore balance, and evolve the planet. It represents a synthesis of some of the world's best personal mastery practices and paths. It focuses on developing long-ignored innate feminine capacities and balancing and integrating them with traditionally masculine resources.

Before we introduce the framework, let's look at how leadership has evolved over the course of human history.

THE ROOTS OF MODERN LEADERSHIP

The roots of modern leadership lie in conflict, territorialism, and the brutal exercise of power. The innate masculine appetite for hunting, conquering, owning, and subjugating appears as a bloody thread running through most expressions of leadership throughout history. Think of Alexander the Great and his dream to conquer the world; Julius Caesar and the empire of Rome; Henry VIII and his impact on English history. They were considered the great leaders of their time, and naturally they were all men. They are invariably depicted in portraits as very severe, aggressive, unhappy, and serious.

Even in most indigenous cultures and tribes, the mantle of leadership was awarded based on a person's (usually a male's) ability to win wars and protect their people from aggressors. India's grand mythological teaching epic, the Mahabharata, is the story of a great war between two sets of male cousins. The cousins look for leadership lessons on how to rule over their subjects from Bhishma, the venerated patriarch who lies (and dies) on his bed of arrows on a colossal battlefield—a battlefield that wrought such destruction that it brought to an end an entire *yuga* (epoch).

The discourse he gave is still venerated as a "how-to" manual for kingship in peacetime, as is *The Art of War* by Sun Tzu, an ancient military treatise used even today by many leaders. The war has moved from the killing fields to business boardrooms and political chambers.

Of course, there have been leaders in history who did not operate from a dominantly masculine orientation. The leaders who have truly transformed and brought lasting positive change to the world embodied a blend of masculine and feminine virtues and capacities. Think of beloved leaders such as Abraham Lincoln, Mahatma Gandhi, Martin Luther King Jr., and Nelson

Mandela. Each had a transformative effect on the world that existed in his time, and each blended tremendous strength with a great capacity for love and care. Lincoln blended masculine traits such as strength of purpose and tenacity with feminine ones such as empathy, openness, and the willingness to nurture others; this capacity was seen as "central to his practice of great leadership."[1] As Leigh Buchanan wrote, "Lincoln's humility and inclusiveness made possible the 'team of rivals' described by Doris Kearns Goodwin in the popular book of that title. Generous and empathic, he made time for people of all stations who approached him with their troubles."[2]

Contrast the legacies of these leaders with those of despotic twentieth-century leaders such as Hitler, Stalin, Mao, Mussolini, Pol Pot, and others. They represented the worst instances of unbridled masculine energy run amok, and nearly destroying human civilization in the process.

Traditional Leadership Models

The traditional leadership model was designed for combat and competition, with a focus on survival, conquest, and defeating the enemy. Traditional leadership is hierarchical; rank determines power and authority. Decisions are made top-down and follow standard procedures, and drill, discipline, and unquestioned compliance are seen as key to achieving goals. A willingness to sacrifice is seen as key to winning, while ends are believed to justify the means. By some measures, this very masculine leadership model has been successful; it has certainly endured for a long time. The positives associated with masculine leadership include discipline, focus, and extraordinary achievements under duress—but, far too often, it comes at a painfully steep human cost.

Today, the context has changed dramatically and with it our expectations of leadership. Leadership was about maintaining order; today, it's about knowing how to navigate ambiguity. In the past, many things were centrally controlled; today, we operate with peer-to-peer networks. We used to have very limited access to information; now, we have universal and instant access to massive amounts of information, to the point of information overload. Power was closely held and is now distributed; we're moving from ranked hierarchies to unranked "heterarchies." The leader was the unquestioned boss, powerful and controlling; now, the leader needs to be a catalyst, empowering and inspiring.

Most current leadership models are essentially behavioral (telling us how to behave as leaders), and thus operate from the outside in. They require us to develop certain competencies as a leader. Some of them also emphasize values and beliefs, which goes one level deeper — but still not deep enough.

Getting at the Source

To manifest leadership based on true power, you need to start with the source. You need to understand what that source is, how to get in touch with it, how to harness it, and how to uniquely manifest it in the world. This is a three-step process: step in, step up, and step out. In the process, you source Shakti, embody Shakti, and, finally, manifest Shakti.

Step in is about stepping into your Shakti, awakening to your deeper being: the source within. It is about connecting to your deeper self, and, through that, to the infinite power of the universe.

Step up is about doing: polishing your life and leadership skills, and embodying a natural balance of masculine and feminine qualities to become a flexible, comfortable leader anchored in personal power.

Step out is about being sensitive to the needs of the context and choosing where and how to best serve in the world. It is about fully manifesting and deploying the Shakti that you've found by asking: What is my unique purpose? What am I here to give life to?

Shakti Leaders Speak: Staying Connected to a Source

For Lynne Twist, effective leadership has to do with staying connected to a source, which we call Shakti:

My relationship with leadership is to stay connected to a source. There is an energy or taproot that is always waiting for our attention. It's always there. It doesn't come and go; we come and go. That taproot is like an expression of God or love. It's not you or me; it has no "either/or" in it; it's you and me. People ask me, "How do you do so much?" or "Don't you get burned out?" and I say to them that burnout to me is being disconnected from source. It doesn't have anything to do with working all night or having too much on your plate. When you're in the zone, your energy is almost limitless. I know that when I'm really, really effective, I'm tapped into something other than my own ego or my own talent or my own intelligence. I'm tapped into being a useful instrument of something that wants to happen. It shows up when you're completely present, when there's a committed listening in the room and committed listening from the leader.[3]

SHAKTI LEADERSHIP

Shakti Leadership is an adaptation of the conscious leadership model developed by a group of facilitators and coaches in India called ChittaSangha (Consciousness Collaborative).[4] The conscious leadership model is about leading with depth, starting from the inside out. It is an approach to leadership that originates from consciousness, the ultimate source of everything. By tapping into that source, we can cultivate a state of being from which comes what we call presence—a state in which you're not preoccupied with the past or future but are completely at home in the moment.

When you are not present, you operate with conditioned knee-jerk responses, making unconscious, default choices. When you are fully present, you're able to see and sense things about the situation clearly, act accordingly, and be fully attuned to all its possibilities.

From a state of presence anchored in consciousness, you can readily access and develop the three essential capacities of leadership: wholeness, flexibility, and congruence. These are the critical capacities from which flow all the qualities and behaviors you need to be an effective leader.

Once you develop these three capacities as a leader, all the behaviors and competencies you need to cultivate will be anchored on solid ground. Without such anchoring, no amount of training in "what good leaders do" can have lasting impact.

It matters whether people manifest behaviors from the conditioned ego self or the deeper, true "ground of being." Only leadership that originates from the fertile ground of your consciousness can sustainably generate the outcomes that your organization and people need. Without that, it is like planting cut flowers and expecting them to grow.

Capacity for Wholeness

Wholeness is the ability to balance, integrate, and unite all the divided and fragmented parts of oneself. Wholeness is emphasized in all major wisdom traditions. It is about healing the many splits that are within all of us.

We think of ourselves as just one person, but we each carry multiple selves within us. Women have a mother-self, a daughter-self, and also an inner man within. Likewise, men have a father-self, a son-self, and an inner woman within them. We are all human beings and we are also divine beings; this split, too, has not been reconciled for most of us. To become whole, we need to bring about a kind of "holy family reunion" within our beings. In a sense, it's about becoming your own mother or father as well as your own beloved. We need to learn how to access and express all these selves within us as appropriate.

The Western view of wholeness is *psychological*, reflected in Carl Jung's insight that we have an ego-self and a shadow-self.

To become psychologically whole, we need to integrate the two. Jung famously said that this was the apprentice piece in the journey to individuation; the "masterpiece" is to integrate the anima and animus—your masculine and feminine dimensions. When you can hold all those pieces together in a coherent way, you have achieved psychological wholeness.

The masculine tendency is to be more self-oriented, while the feminine tendency is to be more other-oriented. When unconscious, the masculine nature can be selfish; when made conscious, this drive leads to individuation. When unconscious, the feminine nature can be submissive; when made conscious, this drive leads to self-transcendence. Individuation and self-transcendence are two sides of the same coin: the mark of a full-blown presence.

From the yogic tradition comes the idea of *spiritual* wholeness—you have to unite the human or ego self and the divine or higher self. It recognizes that you are not only the ego, but also the soul, the *atma*. Ultimately, even the soul has to unite with the supreme soul, *paramatma*.

Chinese or Taoist wisdom focuses on *ecological* wholeness: balancing complementary energies, the yin and the yang. Chinese medicine is about understanding that your energies need to be balanced with the energies of your ecosystem, which creates a state of health. Likewise, every organ in your body is in a yin-yang energy balance with another.

Becoming a whole person requires us to reclaim our lost parts. The three traditions have worked out pieces of the puzzle; now we can reach for a grand integration.

When you become whole, it creates a great sense of joy and releases extraordinary energy—the positive energy of Shakti. The positive and negative poles of a battery are of no use without each other; they need to be connected for energy to flow. Likewise, we are disempowered when we are internally fragmented. Shakti is the energy locked in those poles which can now be released.

Shakti flows and grows from wholeness. Far from being a static, resting state, wholeness is a state of powerful dynamism. When we become whole, Shakti is awakened and active and available in its full power.

Shakti Leaders Speak: On Leadership and Balanced Respect

Author and educator Judy Sorum Brown provides insight into why we need to invite more feminine qualities into leadership:

Men and women who struggle to lead in healthy ways recognize in themselves and others the hunger for a balance of the two orientations in their own lives, relationships, and organizations. . . . Some organizations seem to inadvertently dampen and discourage the feminine dimension in men and women. As a result, those organizations end up dismissing the feminine energies.

It is not easy to have a balanced respect for the dance between masculine and feminine in organizational life, at least in Western culture. Work cultures schooled in one (the masculine, for instance) but unconsciously yearning for the other (the feminine) may swing between them rather than center to hold both. . . . In work cultures that are historically feminine, it may be necessary to explicitly invite the masculine dimension into the leadership.

How do we create conditions in which both the feminine and the masculine perspectives are invited, valued, celebrated, and heard? Leadership is holding both sides and valuing both. It is the precise, disciplined and curious scientist and the aware and gifted storyteller. . . . The feminine is needed not because it trumps the masculine, but because it has been missing from the necessary partnership of the two leadership dimensions.

Leaders create conditions that are either enlivening or deadening. In a sense, leaders—like architects or designers—create emotional space, thinking space, and working space. Our ability to serve as leaders has much to do with how we work with the materials before us. Among the resources are the energies of the feminine and masculine dimensions within us and around us. In a sense, we're trying to create a fire—the release of human energies.[5]

Capacity for Flexibility

The second essential leadership capacity is flexibility. Shakti Leaders need to know how to flex between masculine and feminine energy as the situation or context requires. Most of us tend to get stuck in one mode and don't how to cycle to the other. That's the habitual nature of the mind. Yoga and Chinese martial arts and techniques such as Tai Chi and Qi-gong can be quite beneficial to help overcome this; when you make the body flexible, the mind becomes flexible as well.

The bamboo tree is a great symbol of flexibility. It is able to bend and sway as conditions demand, but does not break, no matter how harsh the wind. The bamboo has become central to many sacred traditions for good reason, as it embodies uprightness and tenacity, elegance and simplicity.

Being flexible when you are *not* operating from presence can be disempowering and come across as being weak, indecisive, or lacking personal conviction as a leader. But if you are in presence and holding your center, you can exercise needed flexibility without any loss of power.

Capacity for Congruence

The third leadership capacity is congruence. When we are congruent, everything is lined up: we are centered, authentic, and aligned. Everything comes together and is moving in harmony with one's *swadharma* (a Sanskrit word for the concept of a personal higher purpose, what one is here to live and be and do). Leaders who are congruent are not pulled in multiple directions. They are aligned with their purpose internally (how they feel) as well as externally (how they act). If you cultivate inner congruence, you will exemplify it on the outside as a highly effective and engaging leader and human being. When a person is congruent, they manifest great integrity; you see them living the truth of who they are, not pretending to be anything else. Congruent people are inspiring to be around; they are powerful beings whose energy comes together into a concentrated force of nature.

Manifesting Love at Work

Love is a word that is finally emerging from the corporate closet. For too long, business has been run purely on self-interest, leaving aside the equally powerful human need to care. Bringing caring or love into the workplace is an inevitable by-product of embracing Shakti Leadership. In fact, it is already happening at conscious companies—and not just because it seems like a nice thing to do. Ron Shaich, founder and CEO of Panera Bread, believes that "Love is a competitive advantage. When you can give voice to and capture love, you can activate all kinds of things in people which is way different than the model which says they should show up and we will pay you $X per hour. You don't have to make a business case for love."[6]

Shakti Leaders Speak: Leading from a Place of Love

Leaders often face situations where they are challenged to stay true to leadership rooted in love. Casey Sheahan, former CEO of Patagonia, recalls:

About two years after I became CEO of Patagonia, we were hit with the global economic crisis. All business leaders at that time were looking with great fear to the future: that business might dramatically slow down; that we might go into a depression; that sales and orders and all business would be negatively affected. I was having meetings with my executive team and with the owners of Patagonia trying to figure out what to do next. The first inclination in traditional businesses is to cut costs. The biggest area of cost for most companies is payroll and overhead. I thought, "Business is going to be tough. We may have to lay some people off." I didn't want do that, because Patagonia is my family and I think of every individual there having children in school and mortgages and car payments. I was really anguished about it. I came home that night after having these discussions at work and talked to my wife at the time, Tara. She said, "Are you making these decisions out of love or fear?" I said, "Fear, of course. Business could get bad and I don't know what's going to happen, but we need to batten down the hatches and tighten the belt and get ready for a really rough ride." She said, "What would happen if you looked at this from a place of love?" I said, "I would not let anybody go. I would find other ways to save money. I would have the workers and sales associates in the stores do the window washing and the cleaning instead of laying off a bunch of people." Well, that's the course I took. Simultaneously, we were introducing our beautiful new product line for a snowy winter, and sales went through the roof. They continued to escalate and the company started growing exponentially from that moment forward for the next five years—and is still growing like that.

In that moment, I could have taken the traditional fear-based path of saving money, trying to do the best thing for the income statement and the balance sheet, or I could think of creative ways to save the jobs of people who are part of this family. They were very appreciative, knowing that they might have lost their jobs. They worked even harder, and pulled together very collaboratively in a creative way to get through the economic crisis. Patagonia came out of the downturn gaining market share and becoming a much more powerful company than it was before. That's the biggest expression of the two energy paradigms that are at work in organizations; which one you follow could determine whether things work out for you in a positive or negative way.

When I took the love decision and made the love choice, I sensed a shift in my consciousness, a shift in my energy. I felt in myself a sense of calm and relief after making that decision. But I was also quite excited to be able to use my mind and work with my team to develop solutions that were creative and we knew hadn't been done before, so it became actually a very exciting time.[7]

For many leaders, "love" seems like something soft — somehow at odds with the steely chill we associate with hardened business-men. Stakeholder theory pioneer and Darden School professor Ed Freeman is blunt on the subject: "In the academic literature, business is about macho crap. Business theorists are embarrassed to hear people talk about love and care and that kind of stuff."[8]

What many leaders fail to recognize is that there is great strength in love. Love is not the sentimental, pink-hearted cartoon that many envision; it brings people together in a real way. For John Mackey, co-founder and CEO of Whole Foods Market, "Love is the most powerful energy in the world. When you have that, you're not weaker; you're actually a lot stronger. That's the narrative that's missing out there and needs to be told."[9]

There is nothing incompatible between love and capitalism. Fred Kofman, author of *Conscious Business: How to Build Value Through Values* and now vice president at LinkedIn, has said, "Because love is a competitive advantage in a free market, the companies that best embody love and that best support the well-being and development of all stakeholders will win. They will accumulate wealth and power and size. Freedom privileges those who are willing to offer the most while drawing the least resources from society. It allows loving people to win over those who are less conscious."[10]

LEADING FROM SHAKTI

Shakti Leadership is not about using people for your objectives, but about serving them and being a good steward of their lives. It's a very different way of looking at leadership. Shakti Leaders don't try to "manage" people; they attract followers because people know that the leader is aligned with a force for good and truly cares about them as human beings.

Shakti Leaders Speak: On Caring

Ping Fu survived the Chinese Cultural Revolution and went on to write the harrowing memoir *Bend, Not Break*. She is now vice president and chief entrepreneur officer of 3D Systems. Here is how she describes her approach to leadership:

I think the reason people follow me is partly ethical; we share the same values and vision of why working on a particular project is worthwhile. But it is also because people know that I care about them—their well-being, their career, their happiness beyond their job, the totality of the person. This is something that came to me naturally; I have a strong mother instinct. When I came to 3D Systems, my boss said, "I am the father and you are the mother." I think a big part of the reason is because I became a surrogate mother to my sister when I was eight years old (during the Cultural Revolution). So I developed the skill of being a mother in my formative years. A mother always wants her children to do well and always cares for her children. Being proud of your children is your biggest reward as a mother. My leadership style is kind of like that. People who work for me sincerely feel that I really care about them, and, when they do well, I'm really proud of them.

I don't believe in cracking the whip. I think what works is setting clear expectations and holding people accountable. I get people to set their own objectives; they own their goals and they own the measurement. That's the tough-love part of leadership. I do that routinely because I don't like to micromanage. People can make mistakes, of course. But if they purposely engage in behavior that negatively affects the entire team, we talk about it. Nobody likes to be shamed or feel like they are the bad apple in the basket. I don't need to crack a whip—if they let other people down, they whip themselves.[11]

Why lead with Shakti if you are a conscious person and leader already? Being conscious would imply that the Shiva consciousness is awakened to a fair degree in you. You are more self-aware and have the ability to deeply reflect on your choices and the impact they have in the world. However, if you wish to bring about real and lasting positive change, you're going to need the agency of Shakti, the power that fuels such change. In yoga, this power is deeply respected, sought, and brought to bear upon situations, for it alone fashions the transformations necessary. We can be highly conscious leaders, but without Shakti we will not be able to achieve the change and transformations needed at these critical times. This transpersonal and higher power alone can bring about the paradigm shifts needed.

As the expression goes, with great power indeed comes great responsibility. Conscious leaders exercise power with great care. Their integrity and intention are tested often; Shakti is theirs only as long as they have self-mastery over their ego and are in selfless service to the greater good.

Shakti Leadership requires that you cultivate deep and consistent presence as a leader. From that place of presence you connect to the Shakti within and are empowered by it. From this Shakti you're able to develop the three essential capacities: wholeness, flexibility, and congruence.

In this chapter, we introduced the broad framework for Shakti Leadership. In the next chapter, we'll take a closer look at the master key: presence.

3

PRESENCE: THE
MASTER KEY

The starting point of accessing Shakti is presence.

Shakti Leaders must undertake a heroic journey—one we'll cover in more detail in later chapters—to come into their full power as leaders. How can we journey consciously with ease and grace, instead of having to suffer through pain, crises, and chaos? The short answer is that we must prepare for the journey by learning how to get out of our ego and into presence.

When you're in presence, you gain access to the power of presence, which is Shakti. Then leadership and followership become natural and seamless, because a transcendent power is now leading the show rather than an individual leader.

As we described earlier, the crisis we collectively and individually face is one of leadership and of consciousness. To overcome this crisis, we must first journey within ourselves to discover the wisdom and answers that are to be found inside our own being. To do this, we must first cultivate presence, a state of being in constant and conscious contact with one's true/higher self and the source of our Shakti. When we are in presence, we become fully aware of and accept whatever is going on within us—our resistances, sorrows, and fears. This mysteriously awakens a deeper capacity: our latent Shakti, through which we gain access to emotional and mental resources within.

Presence also helps us discover our true purpose and find "meaning in our suffering" (as Viktor Frankl put it). This is a critical piece required to reframe any crisis and recognize it as an opportunity for growth. If we are not able to invoke presence in face of a crisis, we will likely succumb to despair.

What Is Presence?

We define presence as a profound sense of present moment awareness: a state of conscious flow where one experiences balance, completeness, connection, and contentment, both internally and in relation to the larger systems of which one is a part. It is a state of being in constant and conscious contact with one's higher self while remaining in flow with all that is.

Presence is what Joseph Campbell described as the navel between heaven and earth.[1] Presence is that sweet spot where you are in the world but not of it; you are connected to something beyond it.

The gifts of presence are the capacity to feel whole, flexible, and congruent.[2] While the gifts don't materialize automatically, you must have presence to cultivate them.

Most of the time, we are not in a state of presence; we are absent, simply not here. The only present is this moment right now. It's only in this present "now" moment that any real thought or creative action can take place. Nothing else exists; the future hasn't happened, and the past is over. The present moment is the only real moment in which we can gain a clear understanding of what is really going on, what is required of us, what is seeking our attention and what we need to manifest.

What does a state of presence feel like? You are calm and centered and balanced, even if there is chaos all around you. You can enjoy the moment for what it is. For leaders, life never lets up. There is always a new set of challenges to overcome. Presence is the place to be during a storm—in the eye of the storm, at the still point of the turning world.

You simply cannot *be* a conscious leader without being fully present. The leader not only has to look calm but actually be calm for their team and organization. Attaining that state of being takes effort and practice; in yoga, this is called *sadhana*. Presence is a state of relaxed concentration that can be cultivated. It is like learning how to ride a bicycle; at some point, muscle memory takes over and it becomes automatic. With enough practice, you can learn to instantly access a state of full presence at any time.

When we step into our presence, each of us is unique. No two people have the same quality of presence; each person's presence is their unique expression of Shakti. You can only be you; you've got to know that and honor it and not try to be who you're not. If you're an acorn, you can only become an oak tree. An oak tree doesn't wonder why it couldn't be a peepal tree. The beautiful thing is that the more you get anchored in your presence and operate from there, the more joy you experience—joy because that is your true and therefore natural state of being. This natural state of our being is *ananda* or bliss. You are in a state of joy and fulfillment because you know that you're being who you are meant to be.

Executive Presence

Executive presence is a competency that is gaining popularity at many corporations as something necessary for stepping into senior leadership roles. Key aspects of executive presence include confidence, poise, and decisiveness, all of which help convey a sense of gravitas. Communication skills, assertiveness, and the ability to gauge an audience or situation are other important qualities. People with strong executive presence have charisma or magnetism and can strongly influence others. They speak clearly with conviction and energy and they have strong body language and good posture. At many companies, executive presence is a significant factor in determining who gets promoted.[3]

Companies are investing a lot of time and money in training for executive presence. The goal is for the leader to be able to project charismatic self-assurance and have a persona that inspires confidence among their followers. But for this training to have a lasting and genuine impact, these behaviors must be based on the deeper presence. Any training that is not grounded in one's deeper presence and higher self will feel like a graft or mask and will not lead to sustained impact over longer periods of time.

Cultivating Presence

We cultivate presence to get in touch with our wholeness and to realize that everything we need is within us at any given moment and always has been. With that realization comes a feeling of serenity and a sense of confidence. You know that Shakti is always accessible within you; you don't need to find it from somewhere outside of yourself.

How can you cultivate a state of presence? By using the presence practice that we describe below. With enough practice, you can cultivate a state of full presence as your default state, ready to take on anything life brings you.

Relaxed Body

This brief practice is adapted from one synthesized by Vijay Bhat and Hank Fieger, conscious leadership coaches who teach executive presence. It is a quick way for busy, stressed, and rushed people to move into a state of presence.

We begin with the foundation of presence, which is a relaxed body. First, be comfortably seated in a chair with your eyes closed, feet uncrossed and firmly planted on the floor. Make sure your head, neck, and shoulders are relaxed, with your spine straight. Place your palms facing upward or downward on your thighs.

Start by tightening your face muscles, scalp, and entire head and neck area. Squeeze, squeeze, squeeze, then release.

Completely release those muscles until they are deeply relaxed, then tighten your shoulders and arms. Make fists with your hands and squeeze everything very tightly—and release. Relax. Next, tighten your ribcage, abdominal muscles, torso, belly, and all your internal organs—and release. Tighten your hips, thighs, knees, calves, ankles, feet, and toes. Curl your toes in tight, tight, tight—and release. Take a deep breath from the top of your head all the way to the tips of your toes to flush out any remaining tension as you scan your body. Feel your entire body relax.

Even Breath, Clear Mind, and Open Heart

From that relaxed body, you're now ready to move into the next signal of presence, which is an even breath. Become acutely aware of your breathing. Notice whether your breathing is even or jagged and consciously make it smooth and even. Your shoulders should be squared back and your belly soft, making your entire ribcage available for full-lung breathing. Inhale, expanding the chest and ballooning the belly. As you exhale, empty the lungs completely and drop the chest. Again inhale, expand the chest, balloon the belly, and exhale. Continue at your own pace until your inhalations and exhalations feel smooth and even.

The next signal of presence is a clear, calm mind. Once the breath is even, go one level deeper and become aware of your thoughts. Imagine that your brain is dissolving into a crystal-clear lake high up on a mountain, with the perfect breeze and temperature. There is no moss on the surface, no ripples in the water, no turbidity. This is your mind: crystal-clear and calm. Step forward to the edge of this lake and look down. See your face reflected back at you: calm, quiet, relaxed. Your whole being is calm, quiet, and relaxed.

Start moving into the lake now, stepping into the waters of a clear mind, and feeling completely refreshed and regenerated in it until the water reaches all the way to your heart. As the cool water touches your chest, allow your heart to relax open. Feel your physical heart inside your ribcage. Feel a sense of love and gratitude toward this organ that has been a faithful companion to you from the time you were just a cluster of cells in your mother's womb. It's thumping away for you, powering you, keeping the rhythm of life for you. Feel deep gratitude and open your heart. When you open your heart, it's as if you can step in through it and enter a state of pure presence that awaits on the other side. You've now shifted state from the ordinary outside surface consciousness to a state of pure being.

This is your state of presence. You know this when you affirm the following truths. Say, "The reality of this moment is that I have nothing to defend." Imbue it with deep meaning and connection. Take a deep breath and allow your gut to know this truth now. Let it relax. Next, say, "The reality of this moment is that I have nothing to promote." Breathe into your heart and know the truth of this statement. Now say, "The reality of this moment is that I have nothing to fear." Breathe into your head and know the truth of this statement.

Having stepped back from your head, your heart, and your gut into your pure presence deep within you, slowly affirm: "The only reality of this moment . . . is that . . . I am . . . here . . . now." Breathe deeply from the top of your head to the tips of your toes, anchoring yourself in the column of your being, your spine.

Now become aware of a powerful river of light flowing from above. This is the Akash-Ganga (the Shakti that powers the Milky Way) flowing through you as the Antar-Ganga (the river of Shakti inside). It is potent and energizing, with the power to completely rejuvenate you. It moves through your spine into all your internal organs, irrigating your whole body-mind, refreshing you, fertilizing you, energizing you. Any excess discharges down through your feet as you become a channel of this Shakti for Mother Earth as well, irrigating Mother Earth with this river of power. Affirm: "I am Shakti now. I am empowered now. All I need is within me. All I need comes to me."

Sensitive Sonar and Energetic Induction

Holding this empowered Shakti presence inside, radiate it in all directions around you, sending it out through your senses. Resolve to bring this to your leadership as you cultivate the next signal of presence, which is a sensitive sonar. We're often so lost in our own thinking that we're not even aware of what's going on around us. Become consciously context-aware now; develop a sensitive sonar that scans and picks up what's not okay, if something is stuck somewhere or if there's a situation you need to step into. Bring all your senses to bear: sight, sound, smell, taste, and touch. Empower all these senses to become the most sensitive sonar that can pick up all the critical information outside and inside you—information you need to be effective and to be of service.

From this state of sensitive sonar, the corollary is that you become an energetic inductor. Leaders who are fully present have the capacity to calm others down. When you enter their presence, there's an energetic field that inducts you and makes you feel calm just by stepping into their vibration. Feel your energy field expanding outward from you in all directions. In your mind, embrace the persons to the right and left of you and all the people in your space and in your life. You must stay present and help them, rather than getting sucked into their drama. Induct everyone around you as if in a warm embrace into your presence.

You are now fully anchored and empowered as a Shakti Leader. Holding this state, bring your awareness back to this moment in time and space. Wriggle your fingers and your toes. Rotate your shoulders, then relax them. Move your head and neck from side to side and in a circle. Continue to be present; flow with the power of your being. Slowly open your eyes and look around you. Notice what you're picking up and how you're feeling inside. Feel a deep, visceral sense of gratitude.

Being fully present and embodying these qualities is key to our development as leaders. If you can sustain a state of presence for five minutes on the first day, ten minutes the next, fifteen minutes on the third day, and so on, this state will gradually become an integral part of you. Eventually, it will become your natural, default state. The more you cultivate presence, the more you will be able to help people who need it.

Losing and Regaining Presence

How often have you walked into a room and seen someone really losing it—thoroughly stressed out and purely reactive, with no control over their emotions? Before you know it, you get sucked into their state of absence; you too have lost your center. Instead of one person drowning, now there are two! The gift of presence is that when you encounter someone who is completely losing it, instead of getting lost with them, you will very naturally, slowly but surely, be able to calm them down. The power of your presence is the capacity to bring others to their presence. It is a wonderful gift that you learn to give anybody, including yourself.

If you forget the core of who you are and are not standing in the ground of pure being and comfort and being okay with all that is, you can rush into a fight-or-flight survival mode. In this mode, we fear for our survival and fight as if we're creatures being attacked in the jungle. Our instinct is to defend ourselves: "Oh my God, something is coming to attack me! I have to protect myself!"

You might go into your emotional heart, which has a great need to be loved and thus a tendency to self-promote: "Please love me, please like me." You feel like you have to sell yourself to others, or you won't be okay.

Or you might go into your mind and start future-tripping, worrying about everything that could possibly go wrong. You feel anxious about what could happen in the future or fall into shame and guilt about the past. This is fear-based thinking.

When we lose presence, we retreat to these head-, heart-, or gut-based coping strategies. These are the three energy centers from where we tend to be located when we're not present.[4] They are typical of the ego self, which is only concerned with safeguarding its personal interests.

How do you step back from these three states? You do so by using very clear affirmations, as described above. Say, "The reality of this moment is that I have nothing to defend." Bring your attention to your gut and notice how that feels. Then say, "The reality of this moment is that I have nothing to promote." Go into your heart and allow yourself to step back from emotional neediness. Then say, "I have nothing to fear." Check in with your mind and notice that in this moment, regardless of what you think might happen later, that is the absolute truth: there is indeed nothing to fear. Then when you step into the next moment, it will be the truth again. From moment to moment, you can be present. As long as you are present, a whole new space-time dimension opens up for new possibilities. Otherwise you remain stuck in an anxious, reactive mode.

If you only do what you've always done, it's simple: you will only get what you always got. But when you drop into presence, a whole new set of possibilities is now available to you. Therefore you say, "The only reality of this moment is that I am here now." That is the truth. You are a being. That being is here in this space, right now. You are that one consciousness that has manifested in this moment in time and space. You are indeed "here now."

When you affirm, "I am here now," it's not just a set of words. You will deeply and completely feel your whole being getting concentrated, your wholeness in full congruence. Affirm, "I am here now, I am empowered now, I am Shakti now." Remember, you are that. We are all that.

When we connect with the river of presence, we realize that it is like an undercurrent that flows through us that we can go back to and take a holy dip in at any time. When we return to this river of presence, Shakti is flowing through us and we can get every-

thing we need. "All I need is within me. All I need comes to me."
If you are stressed and tired and your body needs sleep, then that's
what you'll get. Meanwhile the conscious energy that's flowing
through you is doing what it needs to do—fixing whatever needs
fixing while you rest.

Develop Comfort with Discomfort

Cultivating presence and sourcing Shakti takes practice. Daily
interactions with the outer world and its challenging issues and
people inevitably create an inner disturbance to our preferred
state of equipoise. As we take in, digest, and give out energy that
is continually being processed by our body-mind, we can lose
presence.

One way to reframe the loss of equipoise is to develop a level
of comfort with discomfort: to be able to "sit with" the churn inside. We can become psychologically and even physically resilient
if we stop fighting confusion and develop comfort with discomfort. Allow and "be with" the state of confusion, knowing it is a
transitory stage, a work in progress. To get to clarity, we must
traverse through confusion. Allow the necessary processing time
and space needed to resolve the confusion and bring it to a place
of clarity. If you can accept confusion as being all right, you will
gradually become more at ease and comfortable with ambiguity. Remember, the psyche is an organic, living thing. Just as we
cannot make a blade of grass grow any faster by pulling at it, or
should not switch off the oven before the bread has fully baked,
it helps to think of confusion and discomfort as birth pangs that
will eventually bring joy and clarity. Resisting and fighting them
only makes them stronger.

Comfort and discomfort are a natural occurrence of daily life
that follow one another. We invite you to apply presence and
breathe into each experience deeply. With consistent practice, a
day will soon come when you may move through comfort and
discomfort with the same ease as you inhale and exhale.

Develop Healthy Boundaries

A critical outcome of cultivating presence is the ability to draw and maintain appropriate boundaries in our relationships. This is a much-needed capability given that most relationship issues inevitably boil down to boundary issues — boundaries that are either too closed or too open. They are too closed if one is playing too much from one's masculine energy and is not emotionally or empathetically available to the other. Being too open is a feminine tendency, predominant in people who trust and share too quickly and get entangled in messy codependencies as a result.

Shakti Leaders Speak: On Clear Boundaries

Caryl Stern has kept her priorities in line even as she has held some very important positions:

One of the things I have been really clear about in all of my roles since I had children is that my job is my job (and I have had some really great, important, wonderful jobs), but my family comes first. That doesn't mean I won't do my job; I'll get it done. But no matter who's in the room, if one of my children calls, I take the call. That's true for all the people who report to me. They all know that if your phone rings and it's your child, your parents, or any family member, just say, "Caryl, I need a minute," and take that call. I have done that at the United Nations; I have done that with leaders of our country; I've done that with leaders of other countries. Once, my children called when I was on a stage. I actually took the call in the middle of a speech, and it cracked the entire audience up. The value has also been letting people know what's important to me. This is who I am; I don't take that off when I come to work.[5]

Much heartache and misunderstanding can be avoided if one steps into any relationship and transaction from a place of presence. Presence gives us the emotional intelligence and wisdom to ascertain the speed and level of trust and discretion with which to enter and progress, while remaining vigilant and responsible for how one is sharing power in that dynamic—all from a place of integrity and wholeness.

Presence helps us maintain emotional awareness, self-control, and sufficiency. It is the foundation for a healthy relationship.

Mental Confines

In India, elephants are frequently domesticated and trained to work. When a baby elephant is still quite young, trainers chain it to a tree so it can't move away. As the elephant grows, they keep the chain tied to its leg. At some point, they uncouple the chain from the tree, but the elephant doesn't run away because the chain is still tied to its leg! It doesn't know that it is completely free, so it remains in the confines of what it was socialized into as a baby.

Gay Hendricks refers to this as the "upper limit problem." We tend to place constraints on how happy and successful we allow ourselves to be, because we believe that is all we deserve. The point is that we can become conditioned to accept limitations on our freedom and growth and potential—limitations that only exist in our mind. It is only when we become fully present to the reality of the current moment that we can transcend such mental confines and move toward realizing our powerful and extraordinary potential for happiness and fulfillment.

TAP INTO GREATER PRESENCE

Presence brings you into the ground of consciousness, but consciousness isn't just a still "being" place. It's not just pure awareness; it is not inert. It is also powerfully dynamic, creative, and active. It has great power. The creative power of presence is Shakti: the power that manifests and creates and preserves and destroys and recreates.

There is a grander flow at work at all times which is extremely intelligent and which is processing every situation and moving it forward. All you need to do is tap into it. Presence taps into the natural flow of energy in the moment. It enables you to sense it and align with it. From there you get a sense of what is seeking to emerge in this moment and what is the right thing to do. Presence allows you to discern the *dharma* (the purpose and significance) of the moment. Ultimately everything is going to evolve to its resolution; every so-called mistake just creates another journey. Our chances of getting it right are far greater if we operate from a state of presence and consciousness than from our usual mode, which is reactive and unconscious.

In the next chapter, we'll take a deep dive into the heroic journey—a way to transform your daily living into your fully embodied life.

4

THE HEROIC JOURNEY

The hero's journey, as defined by Joseph Campbell, is a living work-in-progress around the world. One can say it has passed into the collective commons of the repository of human wisdom. Campbell encouraged this, sensing that his body of work and legacy had far to go; it speaks to so many facets of the human experience.

Soon after we are born, and once we acquire language, the most powerful way we are able to absorb wisdom is through stories. Stories bypass the rational-logical (*logos*) mind and go straight to the symbolic (*mythos*) realm, creating a much more inspirational, engaging, and resonant experience than simply receiving information. Please note that we use the terms "myth" or "mythic" as Campbell uses them: not as something that is not real but as symbols of deeper drives at play in our psyche. We use mythology and stories instead of just science and structure because, as Campbell discovered, "Mythology is psychology misread as biography, history, and cosmology."[1] Mythology is simply a very creative way to express human psychology.

Coming into Shakti Leadership requires undergoing a heroic journey with mythic and archetypal elements. When you reframe your leadership journey as a personal myth, it works below and beyond facts and rational cognition, engaging and activating universal forces within the personal and collective unconscious. This is the most inspirational and empowering way to transform your daily living into your fully embodied and self-actualized life. In this chapter, we bring to your attention some key dimensions and applications of this great body of work—dimensions and applications that are of particular relevance to leaders.

THE HEROIC JOURNEY SUMMARIZED

To cut to the core of the mythic heroic journey, we use a simple four-stage model of crisis-trauma-transformation-gift to describe the process of coming into your own fullness as a leader (Figure 4.1).

The journey begins with a crisis in your life—a crisis that shakes you out of normalcy. The crisis throws you into a different world where you experience pain, suffering, even trauma. As you're coming to grips with this new reality, you must confront your worst fear. There comes a moment when it's just you and your shadow, your greatest fear. In *Star Wars: The Empire Strikes Back*, Luke Skywalker goes into the forest and meets his father, Darth Vader, who represents his own shadow.

Figure 4.1—*The Four-Stage Heroic Journey*

*Facing your worst
fear/shadow*

There is an element of danger in crisis, but there is also a turning point built into the moment. The crisis contains the opportunity. As Robin Sharma wrote, "Behind your greatest fear lies your greatest life." There is no avoiding or bypassing it. The only way out is through; you have to face your worst fear, which is your shadow. In that confrontation, there is great personal growth; something new shows up in your being. A new Shakti gets awakened in you as you develop new capacities and unlock new latent power. Your inherent greatness was sitting within you; you just never knew you had it. Now it's suddenly unfolded and the effect is transformational. The fact that you are still standing after your journey means you not only survived your crisis, but in fact are more powerful and resilient for it.

After this transformation, you return to the ordinary world and your growth continues. The cycle is only complete when you share the gift of what you have learned with the world. The more we give, the more we receive. This gift is mysteriously the very thing that your "world"—your team, family, community, or organization—needs to move to the next level. Only then will you have completed the entire heroic cycle.

Essentially, the heroic journey shows that if you are faced with a problem that seems insurmountable, you first have to grow to a new level before you can find a solution to it.

Shakti Leaders Speak: On Crisis and the Journey

Sally Kempton describes the heroic journey in this way:

Once you ask for help and admit your cultural powerlessness, and start asking where the source of power is, you open yourself to the power that is not dependent on culture, position, or even skills. That essentially is how we discover Shakti. Some of us just come in fully empowered by her. But most of us discover Shakti by not knowing what to do or how to proceed. If you're a leader and you're just kicking ass and nothing is challenging you and you are really good at the competitive game, why would you change? There's no incentive for the

average masculinist person to look inside and find a deeper source as long as the
ego-based strategies are working. The failure of personal power for most of us
and for our society as a whole is really the only way that we start to turn to the
feminine source. It is a crisis that triggers the journey, because now you have to
go look for power in a different way. Our society is at that point; our problems are
so huge and our capacity to solve them is so clearly limited that we are intuiting
that we really do need some kind of miraculous connection.[2]

JOURNEYING CONSCIOUSLY

Is it possible to grow without experiencing a crisis and the sub-
sequent suffering? Campbell's work seems to suggest that one
cannot have a heroic journey without a crisis. But why wait for
a crisis? Until you come to that moment of realization, you will
have to journey in the conventional way. It takes courage and self-
mastery to move past the crisis mindset. Most of us who haven't
really experienced life fully yet are all too human in our fragility;
we will unavoidably experience pain, trauma, or suffering. To
"turn the crap into compost," you must take your past pain and
suffering and use it as fertilizer for your future growth.

One can experience the journey with more ease and grace by
becoming more conscious of the deeper processes and elements
involved, and reframing them. The *conscious* heroic journey pro-
ceeds along four stages: the evolutionary impulse, followed by
dissolution, evolution, and resolution (Figure 4.2).

Evolutionary Impulse

This planet was once water and lava, and then, one day, a plant
arrived. After several thousand millennia, an animal then arrived.
The plant didn't say, "I shall evolve." The grander intelligence of
nature, *prakriti*, evolved it. Eventually, humans showed up. We
alone have the ability to discern the evolutionary impulse of nature and say, "Can I partner with it? Can I now consciously evolve

Figure 4.2—*Journeying Consciously*

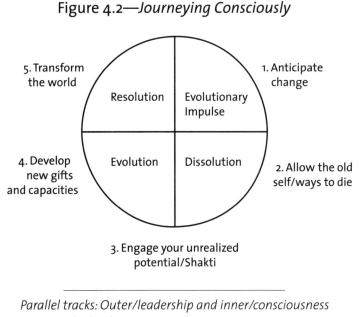

5. Transform
the world

Resolution

Evolutionary
Impulse

1. Anticipate
change

4. Develop
new gifts
and capacities

Evolution

Dissolution

2. Allow the old
self/ways to die

3. Engage your unrealized
potential/Shakti

Parallel tracks: Outer/leadership and inner/consciousness
The leader you are is the person you are.

and help nature along? I, too, am part of nature; I am nature
become conscious."

Inside each of us is the true meaning and purpose of our existence. It is the seed of your life and your being, and carries its
own evolutionary drive and impulse. It's already programmed to
fire and unfold regularly from time to time. However, many of us
do not heed this call to evolutionary adventure. Some people have
let their conditioning stifle them and go against their evolutionary
impulse. Think of it this way: the whole universe is built, structured, and programmed to evolve you, whether you like it or not.
If you don't choose to evolve consciously, it's going to wake you
up through a crisis anyway.

Shakti Leaders Speak: On Evolution's Purpose

There is a growing acceptance of the idea that evolution has a purpose, and
that we humans are agents of advancing the realization of that purpose. One
of the best-known thinkers in this realm is Steve McIntosh, who writes:

Leading theorists are coming to realize that the cosmological evolution of stars and planets, the biological evolution of organisms, and the cultural evolution of human history are all part of a universal process of becoming that has been continuously unfolding since the beginning of our universe with the Big Bang. The advance of evolution encompasses much more than the development of biological species. Indeed, evolution is not just something that is occurring within the universe; evolution itself is what the universe actually is—a grand panoply of micro and macro development that affects everything, and ultimately connects everything.

Once we accept that all forms of evolution—cosmological, biological, and cultural—are part of the same overarching process, despite their significant differences and discontinuities, this leads to a deeper recognition of evolution's meaning and value. And as we begin to discover the underlying meaning and value of evolution, this reveals evolution's purpose.... Evolution is not random, accidental, or otherwise meaningless. On the contrary, its progressive advance reveals the presence of purpose—not an entirely preplanned or externally controlled type of purpose, but rather a creative generation of value that has been continually building upon itself for billions of years.

We increasingly recognize how fundamental values such as beauty, truth, and goodness influence evolution at every level of its unfolding. By coming to understand the "gravitational pull" of values on the process of evolution, we can more clearly see why and how cultural evolution has been achieved in some places and why it has stagnated or regressed in other places.... This new understanding of evolution reveals how both our personal progress as individuals and our collective progress as a society are directly connected to the creative unfolding of the universe as a whole.[3]

Life is never stagnant; it is constantly evolving. Just when you think you have reached a comfortable equilibrium, you will experience some kind of an evolutionary nudge. You think you'll rest a while, but boredom or emptiness will soon set in. Then the call to adventure crashes upon you. Something changes in your actual state or your ideal state. You face a new challenge that wasn't there before, or you sense a dawning awareness that the way things are isn't the way they could or should be. Either way, it is a call to journey, to embark on a fresh adventure of discovery and growth. Learn to recognize that evolutionary impulse and know that it will come. When it does, you will be prepared.

How can you identify false signals? The only way is to apply your best discernment and presence each signal fully. Wait with equipoise, neither moving toward it or away from it. Invoke your Shakti and its wisdom to impel and guide you. Once you wait out the confusion, you will get the clarity of the right choice. Act on it and surrender the outcome to your higher self. Release the hold of the egoic "me" and slip into the flow of Shakti. Trust that even if the original signal appeared to be false, it may now be revealed as true.

Dissolution

A dissolution—some kind of sacrifice or surrender—is going to be asked of you. When you freely and fully submit to it, you don't need to experience pain or trauma.

Journeying begins with a dissonance of the existing equilibrium. The whole journey process is a spiral that's ever expanding upward into higher and higher capacities and levels of consciousness. It always begins with dissonance; something has to disturb the existing equilibrium in order for a new, higher one to be evolved.

As human beings we cling to life, fearing and denying the idea of death. One of the reasons we should make this journey is to remove the negative charge associated with the idea of death. Death is an inescapable part of life. We have to go through it and allow it, for it has many wonderful gifts to give us. We need to let ourselves die to one way of being in order to experience the next and the new possibilities awaiting us.

Anticipate dissolution and allow for the old self or old ways to die, much as a caterpillar has to "die" for a butterfly to emerge.

This is a psychological death that you need to go through. Give in to it. Submit to *thanatos* (the death drive) willingly so it does not come upon you as a destructive breakdown. When you can die to your old self and ways, you come to the place where the next energy to be awakened lies. Detach from the ordinary existence and allow yourself to move into the special world.

Evolution

The evolution stage is where you engage your unrealized potential, your latent Shakti. It's as though there are unused batteries inside you: you've used or experienced one set and are journeying to the next. You find energy ready to be unleashed inside you. In this evolution, you develop new gifts and capacities and discover things you never knew.

Resolution

As Sri Aurobindo said, "All the world's possibilities in Man are waiting as the tree waits in its seed." The resolution stage is where you share your new gifts. With your new capacities, you are now equipped to face challenges and transform your world in some way—whether it's your family, your relationship, your team, or your company.

Even at journey's end, you must remain present and fully alive to the potential that exists in every moment. Instead of being on autopilot and reacting to the churn of the forces, recognize that you've just emerged from a journey and are resting for a while. Anticipate that the lull won't last and change will come again. When that happens, submit yourself to dissolution and allow yourself to die in some way in order to engage once again in something new and different.

Remember that not every journey need be a life-transforming one; many small journeys may come between big journeys. In this way, you evolve and develop other capacities. Those capacities can bring resolution to whatever it is your world is challenged by.

Most of us go through life largely unconscious. Swami Sivananda put it succinctly: "Eating, sleeping, drinking, a little laughter, much weeping: is that all? Don't die here like a worm! Wake up!" Many of us have died like worms many times. That's what gives rise to the yogic idea, also present in other traditions, of the cycle of birth and rebirth. This cycle can also happen while we are still alive in this lifetime. We can be reborn again and again into the same darkness until the light of consciousness starts unfurling and awakening. Then we experience conscious evolution.

THE ONLY WAY OUT IS IN

The very point of the hero's journey is to embrace every challenge as a call to adventure. Change your mental makeup and set forth. Do not surrender to your fear and revulsion; try to see the journey as something of great value, as a gift—an opportunity to become a better version of who you are—and be grateful for it.

Leadership requires knowing how to journey within, knowing how to come into your own. You can't lead anyone or anything if you don't know what's leading you. Your biological and psychological drives direct your personal power until you reclaim it. What are you in charge of if you don't know what's leading you? You've got to know who's "driving your car." You think you're the master of your own life, you think you're going where you're going. But in reality, all these underlying forces are controlling you and you're not even aware of it.

How can we become more aware as leaders? For that, we have to know our inner space and understand our drives. What are our belief systems? Where did we pick them up? Were they ours in the first place? What motivates us? What values are we unconsciously embodying? What's causing our healthy and unhealthy behaviors? What is it in us that causes our outer conflicts and recurring patterns? What within us needs to die or be released? What is seeking to emerge?

Heed the ancient Greek aphorism: "Know thyself."

The hero's journey starts with becoming more self-aware: understanding who you are and what's actually going on in your life. The only way out is in; the only way to answer the call to adventure is to go deep into yourself, because no one else can do this for you. The power, the resources—everything you need to make the journey—are to be found inside you and nowhere else.

The yogic idea of *karma* suggests that this inner work (for which our outer work and world is just an expression or field, referred to as *karma bhoomi*) is something you *chose* to do (or were assigned to do) in this lifetime. You must go through and process particular experiences in this lifetime to evolve and grow in the ways you most need to.

THE DANCE OF THE FIVE ELEMENTS

Yogic wisdom sees all of creation as the divine interplay of the five elements from which it is made: earth, water, fire, air, and space. Each of these elements has its unique movement, emotion, quality, and nature. All systems continuously cycle through these elemental energetic states.

The heroic journey maps onto the cycle as well. The crisis is akin to leaving the familiar groundedness and engagement of earth, to get swept into the fluidity and uncertainty of a state of water. Meeting your greatest fear and experiencing death is like having to go through fire. Emerging out of that, like a phoenix reborn, you can fly free and easy in the element of air. All this takes place within the holding element or emptiness of space, which is the state of presence.

As we know, energy can neither be created nor destroyed; it just transforms from one elemental state to the next. The freedom and ease of a stable being state like air or earth—last until it is time to evolve and journey again—to be taken over by water and fire, again and again.

Recognizing these archetypal elemental energies that are at play at any given time and aligning with their formidable Shakti helps us maintain a state of dynamic equilibrium. We can leverage them to change and evolve without experiencing burnout or missing opportunities for growth.

Some elements are more masculine while others more feminine—think of fire and water. How do we dance through them instead of canceling them out?

Working with the organic nature of the five-elements cycle is also a powerful way to achieve harmonious growth as a company or organization. It serves to balance the drive for scale and numbers-driven growth that is characteristic of most companies. The key is to sense the "music" of the moment and align with its elemental energy. As leaders, we sometimes need to change the music or play another element, while noticing the dissonance we may be causing.

Check in and gauge the energy of your own company. Does it remain exclusively in one element, or does it flow through different elements in a balanced way? The company has its own soul; it is a being in its own right. Each company's elemental energy reflects its life stage. Startups tend to have a lot of fire energy while mature companies have more earth or space energy. Culture is a union and dance of the energy of the leader and the soul of the company. The founder's energy is in some way the company's energy. When the founder leaves and another leader comes in, how they dance that dissonance is very important. Over time, the company develops its own strong culture; a leader who doesn't know how to dance with that energy will be ineffective and rejected by the culture.

Each of us may have a preference for a particular elemental expression in our own energy and leadership style. It's important to retain the ability to be yourself even as you cycle through the different elements. Remaining self-aware and staying present is key. Presence helps you dance with and through the cycle of change that journeying entails, in a way that renews and realigns you instead of depleting and stressing you.

JOURNEYING DIFFERENTLY

Men and women journey differently. While the broad strokes are similar, the nuance and the *kshetras* (domains or fields of action) are different. Joseph Campbell only talked about the hero's journey, and his examples were mainly about men.[4] Maureen Murdock, a follower of Campbell's work, interviewed him to understand how the journey relates to women and their development as individuals. He told her that women don't need to make the journey, that "in the whole mythological tradition the woman is *there*. All she has to do is to realize that she is the place that people are trying to get to. When a woman realizes what her wonderful character is, she's not going to get messed up with the notion of being pseudo-male."[5]

Murdock was dissatisfied with that answer because her personal experience was different. She did her own research and wrote a book called *The Heroine's Journey*.[6] Many other such books on women's process of individuation and growth exist today (*Women Who Run with the Wolves* by Clarissa Pinkola Estes and *Descent to the Goddess* by Sylvia Brinton Perera are particularly compelling).[7]

Let's look at how the journeys differ for men and women.

The Hero's Journey

The hero's journey is a quest for power. Somewhere deep inside, the man is not in touch with his own power. In the quest for that power, he attains meaning and understanding. He also quests for wisdom because wisdom gains him power. It's a thought- and mind-based journey. His greatest fear is failure—not being able to accomplish what he set out to do. The resources the hero has available to him are freedom, direction, logic, reason, focus, integrity, stability, passion, independence, discipline, confidence, awareness, authenticity, and strength—traditionally considered masculine resources.[8]

HERO'S JOURNEY	HEROINE'S JOURNEY
• Quests for power	• Quests for love
• Gains meaning	• Gains freedom
• Task and adventure	• Relationships and romance
• Fear: Failure	• Fear: Violation
• Resources: Freedom, direction, logic, reason, focus, integrity, stability, passion, independence, discipline, confidence, awareness, authenticity, strength	• Resources: Surrender, receptivity, emotion, intuition, radiance, flow, sensuality, nurturing, affection, sharing gentleness, patience, vulnerability

Source (for lists of resources): Jason Fonceca, http://ryzeonline.com/feminine-masculine-traits/.

The Heroine's Journey

A woman's journey often starts as a "descent into the dark," triggered by a profound betrayal of love, violation, loss, or death (of her innocent, untested girlhood). She has to grieve fully and lay her old self to rest before she can be resurrected into her empowered womanhood.

The heroine's journey is a quest for love. The domain of her work and her journey is not tasks and adventures as it is for the man, but relationships and romance. When the heroine seeks and finds the love she seeks within her own self, she becomes psychologically and truly free. She sheds the illusion that some external love/r can complete her. Sensing their bondage to the inner and outer patriarch, women want to be the sovereign master of their own lives; they want freedom. When a woman quests and comes into her own inner source of love, she gains that freedom for herself.

While this may seem rather stereotypical, and our feminist readers may roll their eyes, we ask that you bear with us and let the fullness of the narrative unfold. To give you a reassuring précis: to come into our full, lived potential, both men and women embark on three great journeys, or "mythic quests," over time: for adventure, for romance, and for enlightenment.[9]

A woman's greatest fear is violation—the primal fear that she can be violated anywhere she goes. This is what makes her vulnerable. Yet ultimately, it is this very vulnerability that is her greatest strength, as she discovers it is also the opening to self-transcendence, true power, and the great prize of unity consciousness—consciousness that ultimately makes her inviolable.

The resources available to the heroine for her quest are surrender, receptivity, emotion, intuition, radiance, flow, sensuality, nurturing, affection, sharing, gentleness, patience, and vulnerability—traditionally considered feminine resources.[10]

Check in with your own body-mind to see if you're in touch with these energies. Many women today feel as though they don't have these traits anymore because they've had to "man up" in a man's world, especially in corporate jobs. The hero's resources have been valued; the heroine's resources are typically left at home or worse, dismissed as unimportant ("simply what our mothers did") and of no value in the workplace.

Woman can journey for power, too. As hinted at earlier, the archetypal hero's and heroine's journeys speak more to the masculine and feminine within us than to our gender. Men will journey for love as well—and both men and women eventually journey for enlightened embodiment.

THE HEROINE'S JOURNEY SIMPLIFIED

A woman can journey consciously or unconsciously. Let's first take a look at what an unconscious or unenlightened journey looks like (Figure 4.3).[11] It begins with a crisis, which could be experienced as a loss of power, violation, or betrayal.

Figure 4.3—*The Four-Stage Heroine's Journey*

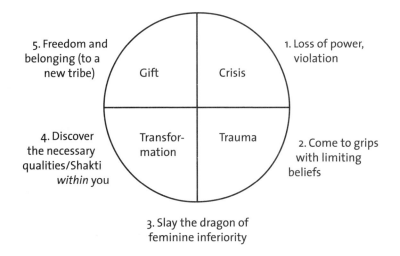

5. Freedom and belonging (to a new tribe) — Gift

1. Loss of power, violation — Crisis

4. Discover the necessary qualities/Shakti *within* you — Transformation

2. Come to grips with limiting beliefs — Trauma

3. Slay the dragon of feminine inferiority

There is a loss of power due to the violation, which is a profound psychological crisis for a woman's body-mind. She experiences intense pain and trauma and is forced to come to grips with her limiting beliefs. Numerous falsehoods have been programmed into her by the patriarchy—falsehoods that she didn't even recognize as false. Now she suddenly wakes up to realize that she's been had. She starts to come to grips with a deeply ingrained and disempowering belief system—one that she didn't even realize was controlling her.

Here the heroine has to slay the dragon of feminine inferiority, the three falsehoods about women that she has been fed by the patriarchy: that women are inferior to men, that women are dependent on men, and that women are incomplete without men.[12] These falsehoods have been fed into women's collective consciousness around the world and have created in them a deep sense of insecurity. A woman journeys to destroy these myths and uncover the truth. She must slay those dragons in order to come through her crisis and her pain. As Murdock puts it, "The dragons that jealously guard the myth of dependency, the myth of female inferiority, and the myth of romantic love are fearsome opponents. This is not a journey for cowards; it takes enormous courage to plumb one's depths."[13]

By facing the ordeal and slaying the dragons, the heroine grows immensely and undergoes a profound transformation. She discovers the necessary qualities and power (Shakti) within her own self, not through the men in her life. She then comes to healing, where she finds her true freedom and sense of belonging and is able to gift that to her new tribe. The whole journey is ultimately about belonging, love and nurturing, keeping the fabric of society together.

When the heroine comes out of the journey, she suddenly discovers other women like herself from all walks of life: the tribe of "happy-to-be-women."[14] It is a tribe of other empowered women who will be able to hold her and support her through her journey in a conscious way. These women are no longer dependent on the masculine and the male parts of society to validate who they are.

So this is the heroine's journey: descent, initiation, and coming into her own power. It's quite different from the hero's journey; death is a critical part of the woman's journey. The woman experiences a kind of death and she has to be able to grieve the loss. These are deep psychological experiences that we have to honor. But that which is true never dies because it is indestructible. Only that which is ready to be dissolved and discarded will die: her surface identity or personality.

Women know how to die. (In a sense, women die every month and are born again through their menstrual cycle.) In the yogic tradition, there is a goddess who takes you to that place when the time comes to die. Named Dhumavati, the great widow, the inauspicious one, she is "the crone goddess of disappointment and letting go."[15] Only when you pass through her do you submit to that complete annihilation, acknowledging, "Yes, I died. I have nothing left." On the other side of the black widowhood—of becoming nothing, so to speak—is the new life.

The Conscious Heroine's Journey: Submitting to the Evolutionary Impulse

The conscious heroine journeys for a great prize: reunion with her inner "holy family" (Figure 4.4). By becoming her own mother and her own beloved, she finds the true and lasting love and freedom for which she has longed and quested.

The conscious woman is attuned to the evolutionary impulse; she lives in the world of feeling and sensing. She senses an aridity, a barrenness to her life, a blocking of the life force and Shakti. She recognizes that it is time to submit to death.

For a woman to mature, something has to die—something precious has to be sacrificed on the altar of death. The good news is that in the grand scheme of things, nothing ever truly dies. However, she doesn't know that when she takes the journey. She has to simply allow, giving up that comfort zone and security and safety of the known. When she allows the death of her childhood, she must presence her shame, her grief, her rage—all that was part of that childhood. Typically, this is triggered by some kind of betrayal or loss of power. She has to presence it, accept it, and see it for what it is, then allow it to process through her: "Yes, I

Figure 4.4—*The Conscious Woman's Journey*

am feeling grief," "Yes, I am feeling shame," or "Yes, I am feeling mighty rage." The fire that's eating her up is the death of her child-hood. Finally, she comes to a place where she can say, "I accept it. I can lay my loss to rest."

Psychoanalyst and author Clarissa Pinkola Estes has developed a very interesting exercise around this idea.[16] She makes her students look at their lifeline and remember a point in their journey where something died—like a river that was going somewhere and was full of life, then suddenly ended, never reaching the ocean. That is a death. Your life energy can get stuck in that moment. For you to really live again, in a new way, you've got to lay your loss to rest and grieve it wholly.

On the other side of death is new life. When you lay your childhood to rest, you have your resurrection into womanhood. You now become a mother to your own child-self. You're not waiting for anyone else to save you, nurture you, or take care of you; you are now taking care of yourself. Just like you would never let anyone violate your child, you will never let anyone violate you again. (We are referring to psychological strength, not to physical strength, which may be overpowered by an aggressor who has more.) That is what it means to become your own mother.

Imaginal Cells and Humanity's Test

Imaginal cells carry the higher evolutionary potential of a species in the body of individuals in that species.[17] Nature is not concerned with whether one individual lives or dies, but continually probes for the overall resilience of an entire species. If a species meets the test, it is resilient enough to survive and thrive and to go on in its evolution. When the time comes for a species to be tested in order to establish its place in the evolving ecosystem of nature, the imaginal cells create enough of a critical mass to unfold the new capacity that gives it the resilience needed, to stay on and thrive and contribute to the rest of the ecosystem.

Today, humanity's consciousness is being tested. Are we ready to go from being psychologically immature, infantile children, to becoming mature beings of the species—both as men and women?

FROM LOVE AND WAR OF THE SEXES TO RECONCILIATION WITHIN

What is going on in the collective consciousness of men that there is such misogyny? What impels so many men to violate women? What is this really about? It is commonplace in many companies for the boss to shout and be abusive. This is how many behave in so-called civilized society; scratch the surface and we're not civilized at all. We have no choice but to evolve; we will be eaten by this tiger unless we tame it. This is the grand journey of the human right now.

Humanity is evolving, but for us to evolve we have to become masters of our own power. That power is the libido, with its dual expressions as a sex or life drive (*eros*) and aggression or death drive (*thanatos*). Unless we can master it and learn how to harness and channel it correctly, we are at its mercy; it can be an energy that rules and drives us.

For humanity to come into its power and maturation as a species and not remain stuck in a state of "juvenile delinquency" requires us to recognize that we have been swinging between love and the war of the sexes. On the one hand, man and woman are deeply drawn to each other; the masculine energy and the feminine energy in each is magnetized to the other's. On the other hand exists a need to consume each other. That need, in an unconscious way, can feel like a battle to destroy each other. These are two sides of the same coin; these energies churn us so we can find reconciliation within as to who we can become as sexually mature beings. The woman, through her womb and what goes on in her cycles, holds the evolutionary journey of libido. Making the libido conscious is the heroine's journey—women's work. The man holds the evolutionary journey of *logos* (meaning) and making that more conscious. That's why so many men are into the wisdom quest.

Where is the woman going with all this? She is looking to the awakening of the Shakti and reclaiming her power, holding the physical space of the body while the man holds more of the psychological space of mind.

As represented by the equal and opposite centrifugal and centripetal forces —which keep entire systems from atoms to galaxies in their structures —that which unifies is the yin force and that which separates is the yang force. Together, they achieve the dynamic equilibrium in which the multiplicity of the Creation can be held even as it evolves. As a carrier of the unifying yin force on behalf of humanity, a woman's journey to self-mastery is really about becoming a woman who masters two worlds: the outer and the inner, the collective and the personal, the masculine and the feminine. She knows how to unite both and through that release the force of creation.

As a carrier of the separating or individuating yang force on behalf of humanity, a man's journey to self-mastery is similar, but complements the woman's by guiding the released forces of creation toward greater and more complex forms of individuated being.

It can be said that the former leads to unity or inclusion, while the latter leads to diversity. Together they are evolving the manifold possibilities of this universe.

The whole journey is about expanding and evolving from your "mini-self" to this great grand self, which contains all these energies in balance through the idea of presence. If you are located in your presence, you can allow these drives to churn you without being at their mercy. You become more of who you can be by recovering all the parts of your self that you have lost. The more you regain those parts, the more whole you'll become and the more whole you become, the more you are able to reclaim power and access it in your leadership.

THE ONLY WAY OUT IS THROUGH

There are times when we choose to journey and times when we choose not to. For every journey we take, there may be several that we don't. What makes us choose certain journeys and not others?

The answers could be different for each of us. It could be fear or inertia or a certain payoff you may stand to lose if you disturb the status quo, or it could be a deeper knowing that you are not yet ripe or ready for such a challenge to a fragile ego; you may come unhinged, mentally and even physically.

There eventually comes a time—a choice-point, a moment of reckoning—when the journey cannot be put off any longer. The only way out is through, which is to say: Not journeying is not an option.

Consider the heroic journey of the wildebeest, often captured in African nature documentaries. There comes a time when they must cross a great river infested with crocodiles. The wildebeest have to do it; they have no choice. They plunge into the river and many of them die. But the crocodiles don't stop them from making the journey. The human soul's journey is similar, when it shows up here in this life. Not living is not an option. Not evolving is not an option either. We must grow or die.

Exercise: Where Are You on the Heroic Journey?

Quite possibly, you may be in the midst of a heroic journey right now. Use the following questions to assess where you are and what you can expect:

- What stage are you at? Evolutionary impulse, dissolution, evolution, or resolution?

- Have you heeded the call? If not, why not?

- Have you explored the new world, with all its possibilities?

- What is your deepest fear? What inner demon do you need to slay?

- What is your unrealized potential (your gift/greatness)?

- When you find your elixir, how will you offer it to the world?

- As you explore these questions, what are you learning about yourself?

THE RISING TIDE OF SHAKTI AS SHAKTI'S OWN JOURNEY

Shakti is a universal force, not just an individual force. Whatever happens in your individual life — on your personal heroic journey — is a reflection of a universal evolution of the collective feminine, responding to the overdeveloped collective masculine consciousness of humanity. The whole system is seeking rebalance; the system has become so hypermasculine that Shakti is going to rise at a collective universal level without us even recognizing it as such.

We're poised for a shift in consciousness; humanity is evolving out of a "power over each other" kind of duality to a harmonized internal wholeness and unity. It will be a rising tide that lifts all boats.

In the next chapter, we take a closer look at the idea of wholeness.

5

BECOMING WHOLE

The first capacity of Shakti Leadership is wholeness. By wholeness, we mean the capacity to balance, integrate, and unite all the divided and fragmented parts of oneself. It is the only state from which we can access our full power.

There is an acute quality of aliveness in being whole. The whole is indeed greater than the sum of the parts; when we achieve wholeness in any dimension, we transcend the qualities of the individual parts being integrated, while still being able to express their unique and diverse aspects.

THE QUEST FOR WHOLENESS

Powerful symbols from diverse cultures seed our collective consciousness and inspire the drive toward the fulfillment of wholeness. They show the way to wholeness to inspire us and serve as goal posts to move toward.

The "vesica piscis" symbol comes from the Western tradition and shows two interconnecting circles within a larger third circle. The interconnecting circles represent the polarities of the masculine and feminine coming together. The overlapping area acts as the yoni or womb through which one can move into the greater third circle, which represents the singularity—the oneness, the whole that contains all dualities.

Another symbol comes from the yogic tradition and shows the *ardhanarishwar*, which is Shiva-Shakti integrated, half man–half woman in a cosmic, eternal dance. Divinity is worshipped in this form in many Indian temples. Casey Sheahan, former CEO of Patagonia, was deeply inspired when he first encountered this image: "Seeing that statue inspired me to think about business in the same way, because we all have these traits within us. I looked at this statue and realized that's the perfect representation of how we need to conduct ourselves energetically. We need both sides."[1]

A third symbol comes from the Chinese tradition of the Tao; it depicts the complementary principles of yin and yang in dynamic equilibrium with each other, each containing the other in itself even as they dance together.

Each of these symbols represents the resolution of polarities and dualities into a harmony, a balance, and a dynamic equilibrium: sustainable, but also ever evolving to newer and more complex states of wholeness.

Shakti Leaders Speak: On the Whole Person

John Gray is the author of *Men Are from Mars, Women Are from Venus.* He has thought deeply about where we are headed on this journey of transcending the masculine-feminine duality:

As we are becoming more conscious of who we are, our unique selves, we find that we're not just physical beings; we have a nonphysical reality which we often call spirit or soul. That part of us is neither wholly masculine nor wholly feminine. It is the whole person, whatever unique calibration of masculine and feminine we are. As we have been moving into this evolutionary drive towards the expression of the unique self, and the self-awareness which leads to that, we feel confined by the narrow stereotypical roles that were historically placed upon us because they were necessary for survival. Why were men and women taking different roles? Because there was a partnership. As the spirit evolves, those rules become way too limiting, and there is tremendous confusion of "Who am I?" because we all have access to both sides.[2]

POLARITIES: The equal-and-opposite or complementary elements we experience and integrate on our way to wholeness.

FEMININE/YIN/ANIMA	MASCULINE/YANG/ANIMUS
• Shakti (energy)	• Shiva (consciousness)
• Right brain	• Left brain
• Relationship	• Task
• Feeling	• Thought
• Intuition	• Intellect
• Estrogen	• Testosterone
• Relaxation	• Concentration
• Divergence	• Convergence
• Grace	• Will

THREE VIEWS OF WHOLENESS

Wholeness is inextricably tied into health and well-being. The yogic, Taoist, and Western perspectives offer three different ways to think about wholeness.[3]

The Yogic View of Wholeness

The yogic view of health and well-being is a deeply spiritual one, expressed in terms of self-transcendence. Life starts with the divine or spirit, which is inherently and eternally whole. The spirit manifests in mind and body. Since life draws continually from this spiritual source, illness and dysfunction result from having somehow broken or separated from it. Naturally, a return to well-being requires a reconnection to spirit, the original source of wholeness.

According to yogic philosophy, man has two natures: an ordinary self (the ego personality or lower/outer nature) that lives in the realm of matter, and a divine self (the soul or higher/inner nature) that lives in the realm of spirit. Wholeness involves transcending your ordinary self and accessing your divine self:

this state is always one of health, joy, and freedom. The divine self has the power and intelligence to heal, making the body and mind whole.

Reflections

- How and when are you aware of your divine self?

- How might you access and receive its healing power in your body?

The Taoist View of Wholeness

The Taoist view of wholeness is expressed in terms of balance. The concept of wholeness or the universal order of life is called Tao (pronounced *dow*). It maintains its dynamic equilibrium through the play of two equal, opposite, and complementary forces called *yin* and *yang*. The interaction of yin and yang produces the primal life energy called *qi* (pronounced *chi*). Everything, including human beings, reflects this essential duality. The yang aspect is masculine, active, strong, and rational, while the yin aspect is feminine, receptive, soft, and emotional. In addition, all creation simultaneously contains subsystems (mind/body/spirit) while being part of increasingly larger systems (family/community/ workplace/nature). All these subsystems—small and large, human and natural—and the energy flows that link them make up the full "ecosystem."

For the entire ecosystem to be healthy and whole, yin-yang balance needs to be maintained within and between systems. The Taoists see illness as an obstruction or stagnation of the flow of qi, which is associated with the imbalance of yin and yang. Wholeness and health are restored when yin and yang are rebalanced and the free and optimum flow of qi is enabled, both within a person and within the ecosystem. This can be done through different energy-work tools and techniques: in medicine, through a balance of herbs, and, for personal equilibrium, by practicing Tai Chi and Qi-gong.

Michael Gelb, author of many books including *How to Think Like Leonardo da Vinci*, has studied Taoist wisdom extensively. He says, "The wisdom of the yin and yang is the balance and harmony of the opposites. It's the very principle that sustains and nourishes our existence. You breathe in, and you breathe out. Your heart expands and contracts. All your cells expand and contract. What we call 'health' is the rhythmic pulsation of our whole being."[4]

Reflections

- What ecosystems are you a part of and how balanced or polarized are they?

- How balanced or polarized are your yin (feminine) and yang (masculine) aspects?

A Western View of Wholeness

In most fields of Western thought, the concept of wholeness is hard to find. Much of Western thought has been directed toward specialization, focusing on individual parts rather than on the whole. This approach has propelled the world's knowledge forward in myriad directions. But it can be limiting and exclusive rather than expansive and holistic.

The most compelling Western concept of wholeness comes from Carl Jung's work on the *ego-shadow*. We each have a shadow or dark side, which consists of our denied, disowned, rejected, or repressed parts. If we don't recognize this, it can hold us back from realizing our true potential. If we do not become conscious of the unconscious, it can rule our life. As Jung said, "The psychological rule says that when an inner situation is not made conscious, it happens outside, as fate."[5] This also holds us back from truly connecting and collaborating with people around us; as the expression goes, "We judge in others what we deny in ourselves."

Jung took the ancient understanding of man as composed of *psyche* (mind) and *soma* (body) one level deeper. He discovered that the psyche itself was composed of multiple aspects, including *ego* and *shadow*. A person's ego is his sense of self or personal identity, the part of himself he is aware or conscious of; this ego is based upon his upbringing and experiences, as well as his aspirations and choices. Each person also carries a "shadow" within the psyche that he is unconscious of; this shadow self is composed of qualities that are the opposite of what is displayed by a person's ego. Deeper wisdom reveals that nothing is true without its exact opposite also being true; thus the universe seeks equilibrium.[6] The way to cultivate wholeness is by embracing the shadow. While the ego does its utmost to deny, reject, and repress the shadow qualities because it judges them as undesirable or threatening, real growth comes from integrating them in your life. This integration returns you to psychological wholeness, a process Jung called "individuation." This can be done through self-understanding, presencing the shadow, polarity mapping, etc. Shadow work is its own field of psychotherapy that one can undergo with a Jungian therapist.

Reflections

- What do you know and acknowledge about your shadow?

- What aspects or qualities of yourself are you giving up in order to be the kind of person you are at present?

- How and when do you cause yourself/others pain or conflict?

- How can you bring your shadow material into the light and express it in a healthy way?

Jung observed that after integrating the ego-shadow, the next level of integration needed to come into one's psychological wholeness or individuation is to integrate your anima (your inner woman/feminine complement if you are a man) and your animus (your inner man/masculine complement if you are a woman).

In sum, these three great traditions give us three different perspectives of wholeness. The yogic perspective points to a higher spiritual wholeness that can be attained by uniting your ordinary self with your divine self. The Taoist perspective embraces a wider, systemic wholeness that can be attained by balancing the yin and yang within yourself and within your ecosystem. The Jungian perspective calls for inner psychological wholeness that can be attained by ego-shadow and anima-animus integration.

THE HOLY FAMILY REUNION

Another split or duality that exists within our own psyche is between our parent-self and our child-self. As we grow and develop a functioning ego in the world, we learn behavioral and belief patterns from our parents.

For a man to individuate, the primary parent he orients himself toward is his father, the first role model for manhood in his life. Similarly, for a woman, the primary parent she orients herself toward, as a model for womanhood, is her mother. As we mature, the voices of our parents continue to resonate inside us, offering us protection and giving advice to our immature, fragile ego or child-self. According to Transactional Analysis (a psychoanalytic therapy for understanding interactions between individuals), we so internalize these voices that they become powerful, archetypal energies that drive our psychological car. We develop an "inner parent" even as we contain within ourselves the archetype of the inner child, which is the wondrous, playful, creative instinct within the psyche.

As we grow up, we individuate out of our primary relationship with our external parent. In order to come into her own adulthood, and become self-driven and self-caring, a girl moving toward maturity needs to disconnect from her bonding pattern with her mother and find those same nurturing, caring qualities within herself. In a sense, she has to become her own mother.

However, given the patriarchy in which most women have been raised, many have oriented themselves away from the mother figure, denying and undervaluing her essential qualities. This has left a wound in our own psyche—a wound that we need to heal. We can do so by validating, acknowledging, and owning all the powerful capacities of the mature feminine within ourselves. This is called "healing the *mother-daughter split*, the *deep feminine wound*."[7] It is how we become mature women. A man has to do the same with his father-figure, by finding and integrating all the positive masculine qualities within himself.

Having come into adulthood, we are now ready to engage in the next level of integration, the "sacred marriage" of the inner masculine and the inner feminine qualities—what Jung called integrating your animus (if you're a woman) or your anima (if you're a man).[8]

In short, we have to reclaim our lost halves to become a whole person. As we become our own parent and our own child and find both our inner feminine and inner masculine natures in a creative, self-sustaining dance within, we achieve a "holy family reunion" and come into our whole, healthy, individuated self (Figure 5.1). This is a happy state where, our inner man-woman union gives us the ability to exercise "tough-love" and our parent-child integration makes us a "wise-fool"!

The Inner Wedding

The Holy Grail of the quest for wholeness in many mythologies is the inner wedding, which can be understood as a dance of love and power within ourselves. Building on the yin-yang symbol, it depicts the sacred union of the "mindful" woman and the "heartful" man, or "woman of wisdom and man of heart."[9] In other

Figure 5.1—*A Holy Family Reunion*

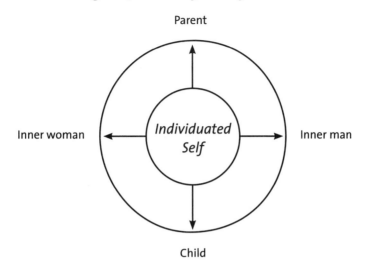

Parent

Inner woman ← Individuated Self → Inner man

Child

words, our own inner masculinity achieves mature wholeness by integrating the complementary yin qualities within; equally our inner femininity matures into wholeness by integrating the complementary yang qualities within (Figure 5.2)

The journey to the inner wedding is a lifetime's work. It takes a significant amount of inner work to discover your complementary other half, to find and meet that beloved and achieve a sacred union. It is about finding your masculine strength and wisdom — the Shiva—as well as awakening the Shakti—the feminine,

Figure 5.2—*The Inner Wedding: A Dance of Love and Power*

The hero learns to say yes, opens boundaries to access vulnerability, and finds love

Heartful Man

Mindful Woman

The heroine learns to say no, creates boundaries to gain security, and reclaims power

emotional nature that vitalizes and nourishes deeply from within. In this way, both men and women become the *ardhanarishwar*, with traits that are simultaneously feminine and masculine; they are each whole, in their own individual way.

Once you are whole, you can enter into perfectly harmonious relationships with anyone because you no longer need them to complete you. When you really come into your individuation, your psychological wholeness, you can step back into the world and know how to accept and include everyone. You know how to "hold the whole" in a way that helps others without making them codependent on you. You know how to hold the space for them so they can journey.

This is the ultimate feminine capacity: to be able to hold the whole and bear the journey of life. Nilima speaks to this based on her own personal experience of the process of individuation and being able to relate deeply to the yogic goddess Shakti.

> I have been on the path of a yogini since the year 2000. My journey of searching began in 1998 with a professional crisis, followed by a personal crisis when my husband was diagnosed with cancer in 2001. I came to yoga through the Sivananda yoga tradition, and then to the Integral Yoga of the Mother and Sri Aurobindo. Since then I have never looked back as I've gone through my journey into the grace of the Mother. Step-by-step, I have turned all aspects of my work, my relationships, my life, my being into the ground and opportunity to do yoga. This is the path of Integral Yoga: to submit and surrender to the supreme Shakti, the bridge between the transcendent source and its material creation, who mediates and integrates the two. Shakti spiritualizes matter and materializes the spirit. We call this supreme Shakti the Divine Mother, or simply the Mother, and relate to her as a child would, finding great joy and strength in a relational and personal experience of a transcendent principle.
>
> The Mother is the agency of the divine that leads evolution to its fulfillment and perfection. As part of that work I, as a woman,

have had to awaken to the reality that in order to grow, a woman has to experience the use and abuse of power, which manifests in many ways, including and especially in your deepest, most loving relationships.

The Dual Nature of the Goddess

The divine consciousness is Shiva, the masculine, and its creative dynamic force is Shakti, the feminine. The goddess in the yogic tradition carries two very beautiful natures. When Shakti is in a harmonized state (i.e., not in conflict with the masculine), she is Parvati or Gauri, which means "the white (or light) one," who sits alongside Shiva with their children Ganesha and Karthikeya. They are a holy family living in harmony, presiding over their universe. But when she has to overpower the masculine that shows up in an unconscious, aggressive, violent way, this same Gauri becomes Kali, the black (or dark) one.

In yogic iconography, a wild, devouring Kali is shown dancing on the corpse of Shiva. A corpse is called *shava*, which literally means a body without Shiva, i.e., consciousness. Only when Shiva awakens and intervenes is Kali, as the chaotic Shakti, appeased and harmonized.

In another yogic myth, the demon Mahishasura (who represents the drive for sexual aggression) is battled over nine days and nine nights and eventually vanquished on the tenth day by the goddess Durga, also an aspect of Kali energy. Durga is a virgin goddess; it's interesting that when the goddess is in her virgin form, she confronts the aggressive sexual force of the masculine. Equally, once that battle is done, she returns to being shanta or peaceful Durga, and reintegrates with Gauri, the happy consort to Shiva.

Such are the beautiful ways in which mythologies from around the world show us the psychology that is at work between the masculine and feminine. It is something that's being worked out in the collective body of humanity.

HEALING THE WOUNDED INNER CHILD

Eastern wisdom and Western psychology both address the different aspects that make up the ego or personality.[10] It is as if one carries within the body not one but many selves, each of which has its own preferences and way of being in the world. To be a well-rounded and functioning person, one needs to be anchored in one's most authentic and aware self, while also being able to access all other parts of the being as required. One such self is the inner child, the self that is creative and curious, with a great capacity for wonder and joy.

This inner child has remained at the psychological age of seven or younger. In an ideal world, our inner child reminds us to have fun, see life afresh in each moment, and be happy. All too often, though, this vulnerable inner child was wounded in the early years and developed coping mechanisms such as tantrums, withdrawal, and self-aggrandizement to deal with difficult situations, feel safe, and get love, acceptance, and security. As we grow up, this inner child can remain wounded; the wound inevitably surfaces when one is under stress or feels threatened. Such situations trigger the memory of the reaction one used as a child to defend or protect oneself, and the same reaction is repeated.

While emotions such as anger, self-pity, or pride may have been useful in difficult childhood situations, they are not usually appropriate responses in your adult life. As an aware adult, you need to uncover your wounds and heal them, thus replacing unhealthy responses with more effective and healthy ones. This will come as a huge relief to you as well as to those around you who have to bear the brunt of your inappropriate behavior patterns. However, even after understanding how negative emotions can impair their health, people are often still unable or unwilling to change. Their well-cultivated habit of negative patterns may still be serving them in some way; perhaps it is the only way they know to satisfy their unmet need to heal the wounded inner child and enact patterns that nourish life and its processes. Connecting with one's genuine needs and learning how to fulfill them in healthy ways are essential aspects of become whole.

Reflections

- What are some of your recurring emotional patterns? When did you first learn them?

- What purpose did they serve then? How are they serving you now?

- Can you identify the feeling under the emotion and the unmet need under that feeling?

- How can you meet this need in a legitimate and healthy way?

The Masculine Wound in Men

The feminine wound is adolescent in nature. Many women today are psychologically stuck at the developmental stage of adolescence, not yet ready to grow into adulthood. They have to wrestle with the myth of romance and dependence on a male figure who will validate her and sexually partner with her.

With men (or the masculine within), we are dealing with an even deeper, more infantile or archaic level of development in the psyche which may have remained unaddressed or incomplete.

Much like our body has an immune system to defend it against attack by foreign antigens, our psyche too has a psychological immune system to defend it against perceived threats to its integrity and equilibrium from an external source. In autoimmune disorders, the very system that protects the body turns to attack and destroy it. Similarly, our hyper-psychological defense systems, if left unaddressed, can stymie our own psychological growth and, worse, make us dysfunctional.

Many men carry a very vulnerable wounded child within and build a formidable defense system to cover that vulnerability. This shows up in some men as aggression and a tendency to ferociously counterattack when they feel threatened. This deep wounding is at work in the collective psyche of men and the masculine within, of which much of the conflict in the world is an expression: violence, wars, terrorism, territorial conflicts at home and in the workplace, power plays, and turf battles.

It is not the purpose of this book to call out the wrongdoing of men, but to compassionately uncover the psychology at work in order to help move it to healthy and more inclusive expressions. The first step is recognition and awareness, followed by taking responsibility for healing and maturing one's undeveloped nature.

With reference to Jung's individuation process, the first journey we must undertake for psychological wholeness (i.e., to integrate the ego-shadow) is to integrate our parent-child selves. The shadow is often a part of our infantile child-self, left undeveloped for various reasons of self-defense. The masculine or inner hero's journey is one of facing our fears and retrieving the shadow or child-self from the unconscious. The second journey is to integrate our anima-animus. This is a journey for love.

Once we have integrated our inner child/shadow and inner beloved, we come into our mature human self and can now set forth on the third journey, the greatest human adventure: the journey into the superconscious, to embrace our higher self, to embody capacities hitherto ascribed to the godhead.

So, whether man or woman, the hero in us needs to quest thrice: once for adventure as we face down our fears, then for romance as we come into our love, and finally for enlightenment, as we attain self-mastery and bring it in selfless service of our world.

THE FOUR-FOLD SELF

The human experience of the heroic journey happens at two broad levels: at the level of the mind and at the level of the body. The level of the mind is called the psyche and the level of the body is called the soma.

There are two forces that each have two sides; one operates on the body, the other on the mind. This creates what Brian Skea called the four-fold self. It is a model of the self with four archetypal aspects: logos, mythos, thanatos, and eros (Figure 5.3).[11]

Humans differ from animals in that we have a mind. The somatic evolution in the animal body, which we still carry, attained a high level of refinement in the course of evolution. In the world of animals before humans, the body became perfected—cats can jump and land with ease, monkeys can hurtle effortlessly from tree to tree. But when the mind came to define what it means to be human, logic, planning, and thinking began to upset the apple cart of evolution. The minute we became thinking animals, we became very confused animals. The body and mind have been in a tremendous tussle with each other inside each of us ever since. The psyche says, "Stay, do the work," but the soma may say, "I don't care. I just want to sleep." We can only become whole and attain physical health and mental clarity to

Figure 5.3—The Four-fold Self

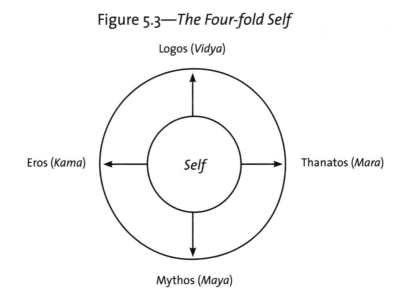

Expanding and Evolving from 'self' to 'Self' through Presence

the extent that we are able to balance and harmonize our psychic and somatic energies.

Different forces are at play in the psyche and the soma. In the soma there is a drive for life, or *eros*. All animals are driven to mate and reproduce life. There is also in each of us a death drive, or *thanatos*. This is also essential. Consider what happens when some of our cells fail to die; that is how we get cancer, because thanatos is not working anymore. Without death, there can be no further life. Where there is a drive for life, there has to be a drive for death. Otherwise, the cycle cannot continue.

A book called *Terror, Violence, and the Impulse to Destroy* was released soon after the traumatic events of 9/11. Psychologists sought to understand what in human nature could cause individuals to wreak such destruction. Where do these destructive impulses come from?[12] They are in our biology. Along with our sexual instinct ("kama" in sanskrit), inside each of us we carry a death drive ("mara" in sanskrit) from which the impulse to destroy emanates.

Our psyche also has two sides: logos and mythos. *Logos* is the logical and rational mind that helps you to think things through, to understand and discern. That is the drive trying to evolve us to the next level of consciousness. To balance it, you have the unconscious *mythos*, which dwells in the mythical, symbolic world, the special world, with archetypes embodying emotions such as lust, anger, hatred, greed, and jealousy. In the yogic tradition, these two aspects are known as *vidya* and *maya*. Logos or *vidya* is considered the realm of the masculine and mythos or *maya* the realm of the feminine.

As thinking beings, many of us would prefer to stay in the upper realm. However, we have no choice but to also cycle through the lower realm. That's where the real power, the Shakti, the juice of life is to be found. It is not found in the unmoving masculine, the eternal, unmanifest Shiva, or its representative, the reasoning mind. It has to be lived and gained by traversing the vivifying, mythic ground of Shakti.

This is the four-fold self. Your body-mind is constantly being churned by these four forces. It's as if we're being turned through these four arms. They are pulling one against the other and we are right in the middle of it. That is your journey.

A UNIVERSAL SYMBOL OF WHOLENESS AND AUSPICIOUS BEING

Somewhere there is only one psyche, the collective consciousness. Whenever it discerns a truth of the journey of life, it tries to put it together in some kind of diagrammatic form. The resulting symbols capture eternal truths.

The incredible geometry and physics of creation have been understood and captured across all the great wisdom traditions in the symbol of the cross, which is closely associated with Christianity but has universally come to signify wholeness and auspicious feeling. You see it across many wisdom traditions, such as the Hindu and Buddhist swastika and in the *chakana*, the "Inca cross." It represents the originating and organizing principles wherein the divine, the eternal, can manifest here on earth. At the center, where the two arms cross, is the portal between all that is and who you are. Standing there is what it means to be centered, to be fully and truly present. The four arms represent the four directions or the four faces of Brahma. The drama of reality and the dynamics of creation and how it works are captured in these symbols from different traditions.

The conscious and unconscious are two worlds: that which you know and that which you don't know. To master life, you have to know how to stand in that still space at the center, the calm eye of the storm. This center is where you access your wholeness, all parts of your humanity. It is where you harmonize and balance, integrate and align with the four main drives required to express yourself as fully human.

Your presence is also located in this center. When you are thus centered, you are truly present.

6

CULTIVATING FLEXIBILITY

Aconscious leader is flexible. We define flexibility as "the capacity to switch modes seamlessly and to bend without breaking, as the situation or the context requires." Examples of flexibility abound in nature. The bamboo tree gets its resilience from its ability to be flexible; it bends but doesn't break in the wind. A chameleon knows how to change colors to adapt to its context in order to survive and thrive. Leaders also need to be able to bend but not break, adapting to circumstances in a principled way without sacrificing their core values.

POLARITIES AND PARADOXES

The constant and inexorable flow of life takes us through a continuous rhythm between polarities, which often show up for leaders as dilemmas. For example, leaders may be faced with dilemmas such as efficiency versus innovation, short term versus long term, urgent versus important, and control versus delegation. The mastery needed to handle dilemmas is the ability to flex.

When dealing with polarities, the choice is not between right and wrong; it is between right and right. It is like being asked to choose between the North Pole and South Pole; there is no good or bad or right or wrong. Yet, we still face the tension of having to make a choice. We have to learn how and when to cycle from one pole to the other, instead of trying to be both. We need to sense what the situation truly calls for in the moment from a state of presence. Some leadership dilemmas present us with a paradox. This is where we have a third option: one of not simply choosing or cycling between the two poles, but knowing how to go beyond them into a third sweet spot. Michael Gelb offers examples of the kinds of challenges we face in reconciling the seemingly irreconcilable:[1]

- Think strategically and invest in the future—but keep the numbers up. Be a long-term thinker, but also think about the short-term.

- Be entrepreneurial and take risks—but don't cost the business anything by failing.

- Continue to do everything you're currently doing even better—and spend more time communicating with employees, serving on teams, and launching new products.

- Know every detail of your business—but delegate more responsibility to others.

- Become passionately dedicated to your vision and fanatically committed to carrying it out—but be flexible, responsive, and able to change direction quickly.

- Speak up, be a leader, set the direction—but be participative, listen well, cooperate.

- Have all the traditional masculine virtues—and all the newly ascending feminine virtues.

Facing a polarity is like being caught between the two poles of a horseshoe magnet. Between the magnet's two poles exists a field that is invisible but powerful. That is your field of potential and creation, created precisely because of the polarity. In such a field, you have the opportunity to convert potential energy into kinetic energy. If you place a wire in the space between magnetic poles, an electric current is generated. The fuel or life force or energy that moves and animates life would not exist without polarities.

POLARITY MAPPING

A useful tool to think about dilemmas is polarity mapping, developed by Dr. Barry Johnson.[2] When faced with a polarity, most people tend to have a preference for one of the choices. Polarity mapping is a powerful tool to help us come unstuck from our either/or thought and behavioral patterns. Many problems are simply polarities that can be handled by using "and" rather than "or"—that is, by including both polar qualities as interdependent pairs in coming up with the solution. Indeed, in many cases that is the only way to find a lasting, impactful solution.

Here is a simple example of a polarity map, illustrated in Figure 6.1. We all want to live and avoid death. For that, we must inhale

Figure 6.1—Polarity Map

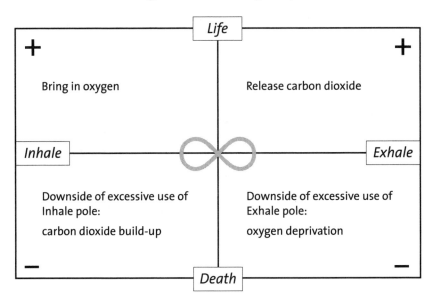

and exhale. Many values dilemmas are like being asked to choose whether you prefer inhalation or exhalation. We attach a positive charge to inhalation because that is what brings life-giving oxygen into our lungs. But if you continue to inhale without exhaling, you start falling into the negative, the excessive use of the perceived positive pole. The downside of the excessive use of the inhale pole is that carbon dioxide builds up inside your body. When that happens, your body automatically moves to the other pole, where it starts releasing the carbon dioxide. If you keep releasing carbon dioxide, very naturally you will fall into the excessive use of the exhale pole, which leads to oxygen deprivation.

This is how you cycle through polarities where both are needed. It's a very natural law: too much of something automatically pushes you to the other side, and too much of its opposite pushes you back the other way again. This is how the rhythm of life is sustained. Far from being bad things, polarities are very necessary. We simply need to recognize where we are on the cycle and respond accordingly.

Shakti Leaders Speak: On Polarities

Lynne Twist offers a compelling way to transcend polarities, rooted in the difference between taking a position versus taking a stand.

When I'm in a leadership position and I'm confused and there are so many voices and you can't tell which way to go, who's right and who's wrong, and whose voice is stronger or louder, I always feel that what wants to come through can't show up. When people get caught in what I call their point of view or their position, it creates a counter point of view. A position always creates its opposition: left creates right, right creates left, here creates there, up creates down, us creates them. Those are positions. Think of them as just points of view . . . like when you have a particular point of view because you're in Washington, D.C. Points of view are important and useful; they're positions on the game board. But if you think yours is the only correct one, that clouds your capacity for change.

A better way to think about this is called "taking a stand." All great leadership comes from taking a stand. A stand is a place from which you have vision. A stand encompasses, allows, and respects all points of view. Once a point of view has been respected or heard, it can dissolve; it doesn't need to fight for its position. When you take a stand, you relinquish your point of view; instead, you can lead with an inspiring vision—something that encompasses and allows all points of view to be seen, respected, and to contribute. Once you receive them, they can dissolve because they no longer need to fight for being right or wrong. In a meeting where people are arguing from their point of view, if the leader can stand for a vision larger than or more profound than any points of view in the meeting, and from there receive, hear, and recreate every point of view at the table, then the arguing of positionality and who is right and who is wrong starts to dissolve, and everybody starts to find alignment and a shared vision. The issue can move forward toward its natural resolution or fulfillment.

Gandhi is an example of a leader who took a stand that allowed all points of view to be heard, respected, and begin to dissolve. In the work that I did with the Hunger Project, we were not against anything. We were standing for a world where every human being has a chance for a healthy and productive life. Martin Luther King Jr. is another example; his vision was what inspired his leadership, not his point of view. Obviously he had a point of view that segregation was wrong; he had a position that the laws that were governing our country were bigoted. All of that was totally valid. But where he led from was vision and a stand, not from a position for or against anything.[3]

Masculine and Feminine Polarity Map

Masculine and feminine values present a similar polarity (Figure 6.2). You may be a woman or a man, but to say "Because I'm a woman I've got to be more feminine" or "Because I'm a man I've got to be more masculine" is like forcing yourself to choose between inhaling and exhaling. These are complementary qualities; together they bring wholeness. They are polarities to be leveraged to unlock and increase the energy available in them for your use, to evolve and raise your game, as well as your ability to function as a whole human being.

Figure 6.2—*Feminine and Masculine Polarity Map*

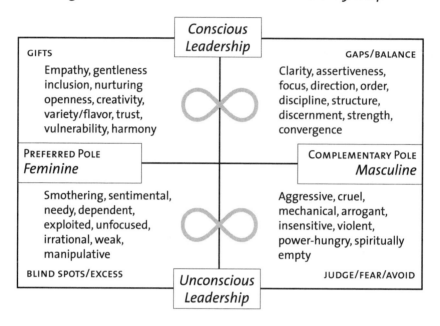

GIFTS	*Conscious Leadership*	GAPS/BALANCE
Empathy, gentleness inclusion, nurturing openness, creativity, variety/flavor, trust, vulnerability, harmony		Clarity, assertiveness, focus, direction, order, discipline, structure, discernment, strength, convergence

PREFERRED POLE *Feminine*		COMPLEMENTARY POLE *Masculine*
Smothering, sentimental, needy, dependent, exploited, unfocused, irrational, weak, manipulative		Aggressive, cruel, mechanical, arrogant, insensitive, violent, power-hungry, spiritually empty
BLIND SPOTS/EXCESS	*Unconscious Leadership*	JUDGE/FEAR/AVOID

Our age of science and technology has overvalued the mind and the rational self at the expense of our creative and intuitive side. Of course, coming on the heels of the Dark Ages, the rational self clearly *needed* to be developed. But by going too far in that direction, we are in danger of losing the other side. It's like going to the gym and only working out the side of your body. We need to develop all these other parts: our intuition, our emotional intelligence, our systemic intelligence, and our spiritual intelligence.

Likewise, masculine energy has been much more cultivated in most of us (male and female alike) through our cultures and educational systems. You can't fly with just one wing. The other side has been largely ignored and devalued. This whole journey — and the central message of this book — is about knowing how to develop the neglected feminine and bring it into an equal balance.

Once you are conscious of such polarities and your own proclivities, you can determine how you need to be in a given situation. Find your dominant archetype, but know what your complementary archetype is and draw from that to flex as needed. Presence gives you the capacity to flex in a way that is not necessarily your natural tendency or archetype.

Reflections

Take a few moments to study the Masculine and Feminine Polarity Map in Figure 6.2.

Most of us have a preferred pole. Let's suppose it's the feminine. We need to recognize it has an interdependent pair, which is the masculine. If we prefer the feminine pole, what are the gifts that are available to us and how do we move toward mastery? There are many wonderful feminine qualities listed in the upper-left quadrant. These are gifts that we start displaying when we are in this pole. While we are in this pole, though, we may tend to neglect the other pole. Or worse, we judge, fear, and avoid qualities of the other pole (masculine) in the terms listed in the bottom-right quadrant. If we continue to neglect our masculine energy, there's a good chance we will get into our blind spot and go too far on the feminine side. Any excess of the feminine pole creates its own shadow, with the qualities listed in the bottom-left quadrant. Men and women alike need to recognize and cultivate the positive masculine values of the upper-right quadrant.

- Which is your preferred polarity, masculine or feminine?

- How can you stop neglecting and start developing the positive qualities of the other?

- What are your early warning signs when you fall below the line, into excessive feminine or masculine energy? Which behaviors do you start to typically demonstrate? Make note so you can catch yourself in time. You need to take prompt action to move diagonally across into the positive behaviors of the complementary pole.

- What are some immediate and easy to do action steps or behaviors you are willing and able to take then? Note them down.

The key insight here is that to be a conscious leader you must stay vigilant and present to remain "above the line," and flex with ease between the upper two quadrants. Otherwise, you risk falling into unconscious leadership and getting stuck in a vicious cycle toggling between the lower two quadrants—an all too common experience.

The Story of the Sagar Manthan

The Hindu myth of the *sagar manthan*, "the churning of the ocean," brilliantly captures the idea of how dealing with polarities can bring the elixir to the surface. The story is set in the ocean of consciousness. Just as we churn milk to make the butter rise, so too we must churn this ocean of consciousness to bring the *amrita* up, the nectar of immortality, which will break us out of our limited human experience of disease, decay, pain, suffering, and death.

In the myth, the devas and the asuras, the good guys and the bad guys, have to work together to churn the ocean. Vishnu, the Preserver and Protector, becomes a tortoise. Mandhara, the mountain, becomes the churning stick, the centering principle around which all polarities move, and rests on Vishnu so it doesn't sink to the bottom of the ocean. The great serpent Vasuki becomes the rope that the *devas* and *asuras* use to churn the ocean. The *devas* represent the positive pole and the *asuras* the negative pole.

As they churn, many *ratnas* rise from the ocean of consciousness, fourteen different jewels that signify *siddhis* or psychic or spiritual powers and are shared equally between the *devas* and *asuras*. Finally, a great big pot of nectar rises to the surface. Here, the light needs to trick the dark, because ultimately this whole thing is a game that the good guys have to win. In the end, the grand design doesn't want the dark to win; the dark is simply serving a role to surface more of the light. What's the point of evolution if everything goes back to dissolution? We need to and want to evolve. The trick that the light plays is that Vishnu assumes the form of Mohini, a beautiful temptress. All the *asuras* are so excited they follow her, leaving the pot of nectar behind for the *devas* to drink and regain with their immortality the kingdom they had lost (how that happened is another story).

The essence of this story is that we all have positive aspects (what Lincoln called "the better angels of our nature") and lesser aspects (our internal demons). They are all within us, and they are churning us. That's the role they have to play, because through that churn we surface the elixir, the nectar of immortality, the truth that will set us free.

Where there is great light, there is also great darkness; where there are angels, there are demons. We must know that and watch for it. Life is a constant inhale and exhale, an undulation between one pole and the other. You have to be present and be ready for the other pole when its time comes. When the churn starts, all that is in the ocean (our unconscious) comes up. This is an important warning: when we churn our psyche or engage these polarities within, we have to do so with discernment and proper guidance so that what comes up does not unhinge us.

ARCHETYPES ENCOUNTERED ON THE JOURNEY

Having described the universal pattern of the heroic leadership journey, we introduce another key feature of journey work: the cast of characters one encounters on the way. These are archetypes; they are agents of our individuation and awaken us to the realization that "No one is our enemy, no one is our ally; all alike are our teachers."[4] Navigating the dynamics each unleashes upon us and extracting the teachings and gifts they are here to give requires great flexibility and agility.

The characters in our journey are reflections of the four-fold self that we described in Chapter 5: eros, thanatos, logos, mythos. These are the main drives, urges, and voices in the unconscious that are in polarized conflict within us and churn our mind and body. Navigating these archetypal powers is supremely challenging and a true test of our capacity to survive and thrive. Emerging through these distills our full-blown psychological and physical resilience, resulting in our coming of age as mature, self-directed humans and leaders embodying our unique awakened Shakti.

We come across thousands of people in our life. But according to the hero's journey framework, it actually boils down to a handful of archetypal characters. As in most movies about human lives, there's a hero, a heroine, a villain, and a helper. If you were a screenwriter, you'd come up with a pretty standard set of characters. Those characters exist in all our lives, but most of us simply haven't seen them that way. They are called archetypes because they are simply the personalities through which a classic, timeless pattern is manifested. It's not really about who they are; they each play a certain role in your life. It's about something bigger than them, a universal pattern of behavior that gets played out through them toward you.

Major Characters

Major characters in the heroic journey include the mentor and the nemesis. The mentor carries your higher self for you, what we could also call your divine self or your soul self. You are meant to mature and grow into a powerful being; the mentor represents that being. He shows up as a role model to guide you.

Just as the mentor carries your higher-self aspect, the nemesis carries your shadow: all the parts of you that you have repressed, suppressed, and denied. These could also be undeveloped parts of yourself. They remain undeveloped and therefore almost infantile, and you recognize them in the behavior of someone who shows up in your life. That's the way life mirrors to you, indicating where your unfinished business lies. It is a part of you that you need to reclaim in some way, that you need in order to become whole, to heal. It could be a fear you need to face. So even seemingly bad guys play essential roles in the unfolding of your potential.

We evolve and become more of who we are when we start recognizing that all these characters are in fact aspects of ourselves. Then we can start reclaiming those parts of us, those energies within us. We start becoming more whole by bringing everything that was in our undeveloped, unconscious, or subconscious self into our consciousness and awareness. Suddenly we have more energies available to play with; we become more flexible, agile, fluid, and capable of showing up in different roles and modes, even as we become more whole. That's how we grow.

People who show up in our lives often trigger us and push our buttons. They are here for our awakening and growth. When we are challenged by such people, we should say,

- What do I need to learn from this experience?

- What about this person's behavior triggers me? In what way am I perhaps also like that?

- Is that something I need to acknowledge instead of deny? Better still, is there something in this denied quality that may be something I need?

- How does that relate to who I am? What part of me is being reflected in this situation?

- What do I need to claim about myself that'll make me a little more whole?

If you remain present with your discomfort and denial long enough, you will eventually mine the gift that is in it. You may discern that you need to create healthier boundaries and gain the power to become more assertive. Or you may find yourself opening your heart and feeling more empathy towards yourself and others.

You grow by making meaning from all the archetypes that show up in your life, instead of playing the victim and feeling sorry for yourself. You come to understand that each person has played a vital and necessary role in furthering your growth.

It is one thing to recognize that your mentor is a reflection of your higher self, but recognizing that your adversaries too have something to teach you can be a challenge. You need to eventually take on some of the qualities you judge harshly in the villain. But in order to do so, you will have to find the goodness in the so-called badness. You have to recognize that the original quality is not in itself bad; it's just showing up in a distorted way. When you can find that quality, the goodness, the golden nugget in that darkness and can manifest it in your own behavior, personality, and being, you become more of who you can be.

Complementary Energies and Projection

When things happen to us in life, we are quick to label them as good or bad, based on how they appear to us in the moment. Just as there is goodness in what we label as bad, there is also some badness in what we consider good. Our value judgments and preferences tend to take one pole and deem it good and judge and deny the other as bad. The minute you choose one complement over its opposite, you create its shadow. Once you create the shadow, it's only a matter of time before it shows up in your life as a limiting factor, an impediment to your growth.

In sum, that which we deny in ourselves we project onto another and judge as bad. For example, if you are a workaholic, what part of yourself, which complementary energy, have you denied? It is probably the part of you that would like to leave at 6:00 P.M. and do some of the other things you enjoy and value. That self has been denied by you. How does it show up in your life? As a colleague you judge very harshly who goes home at 5:30 P.M. every day. Because you have denied it so much in yourself, there's a negative charge attached to that part of you. There's a huge positive charge attached to the "good" workaholic part of you, a nice halo around your head. But the other part of you looks like a fellow with horns, so you distance yourself from that person. The archetypal energy of that complementary aspect of you shows up through the behavior of this one person. Instead of seeing the energy as a mirror, you reject it.

It is startling how often this occurs and how much it impacts our relationships. Most conflicts we have with others can be traced back to a part of ourselves that we haven't fully owned. This is then projected onto another person and shows up in their behavior toward you. Life is giving you a mirror, asking you to look at something and take responsibility for it. When you realize this and take a moment to say, "I'm going to do something about this instead of being a victim of this situation," the energy that was polarized gets discharged. What happens when you discharge that energy to neutrality? You cannot change anyone else, but the minute you change yourself, everything around you starts changing. Once you withdraw your projection from that person, by reclaiming your own denied energy (that they were effectively carrying for you), the other person now shows up as the person he really was all along!

The so-called "villain" can be your greatest teacher, but it's a difficult lesson to learn and can take a long time. Be kind to yourself and don't judge yourself harshly if you haven't been able to forgive. Instead, dig deep and find the endurance to stay with the process. Realize that "one day I will get to love, accept, forgive, and truly move on, and will have grown from this." Indeed, a time may come when you will have learned so much from your "villain" that gratitude will flow from you toward him, not just forgiveness or acceptance.

Minor Characters

Along with the major characters, we encounter a number of smaller role players during the journey.

The Herald

This could be a person in your life whom you have known for a long time, but one day they herald something to you, something that to any other person might feel like nothing, just another trivial part of the script. But there is a message that zings home to you in what they have to say. You're being given a little warning: it is time to get out of the complacency and comfort of normal life. Changes are imminent; things are going to start happening. Your soul is ready to journey.

When the herald shows up in your life, it can be like having a dream or vision. In fact, heralds do often come to people in their dreams. It could happen when you are watching a movie, or when you are stopped at a traffic light and you turn and see a huge billboard in the middle of nowhere that strongly speaks to you. Everything goes out of focus and this message seems to be tunneling to you. These are herald moments. You have to pay attention and recognize these moments when they occur, for it is all too easy to ignore them and miss the opportunity they are pointing to.

Threshold Guardians, Testers, and Tricksters

In many traditions, such as Tibetan Buddhism, masks or statues of wrathful or malevolent deities are placed at the entrance of homes and temples as gatekeepers. These threshold guardians are there to ward off and scare off pretenders. Only the true hero has the courage to enter the special world. The guardian wants to make sure that you are worthy of entering.

The role of the guardian is to test you, to ask, "Are you smart enough? Do you have what it takes to see this through?" Sometimes he can actually play a more subtle role; he may be someone who makes you think you're going a certain way but actually tricks you into another experience. Gollum in *The Lord of the Rings* is such a tester, because you never know if he's a good or bad guy. Is he friend or foe? Should you follow or not follow?

These guardians confuse you and test your resolve to go the distance. In the Indian epic the Ramayana, Shurpanakha (the sister of the demon king Ravana) is a tester; she disguises herself and asks Ram to marry her. He says, "I'm already married, go to my brother Lakshmana." She does, but Lakshmana has discernment and doesn't get fooled. On his heroic journey, he passed the test, proving his worthiness as a hero.

The "Fool" archetype is another version of the trickster as teacher. It reflects the hero's innocence and our inner child-self and reminds us to forgive our stupidity, embrace our shame, lighten up and not take ourselves too seriously. This archetype provides much needed comic relief in life's all-too-serious script. It is why the Sufi path engages and cultivates this fool-self, seeing it as a high road to self-mastery.

The Shape-Shifter

A shape-shifter can be your anima or animus. For a woman, it would be a man who shows up. He may look like a lover but reveals himself to be a villain. She doesn't know if he's someone she should love or hate; he seems to be shape-shifting. It is an encounter with a seemingly "light man" who changes persona and becomes a "dark man." He is mirroring the woman's inner process of integrating her positive animus with her shadow animus. This can be a rocky and unsettling phase in the journey to maturation.

The Goddess and the Temptress

There is, in the hero's journey and sometimes in the heroine's journey, the goddess or the temptress. The positive aspect is the goddess, who is like a great mother. In the yogic tradition, it is the Kali energy: she looks like she's destroying things, but in her fire you can be born again. You feel like you've come back to the womb.

Sometimes for the hero there can be an encounter with a temptress, who asks him to forgo his journey and stay with her. Many years may pass and the hero may completely forget why he started the journey. In the Mahabharata, Arjuna hangs around for ages in a beguiling underwater world with Uloopi, the Naga princess. In the more masculine spiritual traditions, the message is that when you're on your journey to come into your enlightenment, don't get waylaid by women who are described as distractions, nymphs, and *apsaras*. You'll find many such tales dotted through heroic epics. While this can come across as dismissive of women, most spiritual traditions discourage romantic entanglements on the way to awakening. But once the goal is attained, having sublimated the libidinous lower nature and matured into wholeness, the return journey allows and encourages entering into enlightened partnerships.

Shifting Roles

Archetypal forces are actually part of your own personal unconscious, and the more you can make your unconscious your own and claim it, the more conscious you can be, the more enlightened you become. You could fulfill any one of these roles for others. The role played by a mentor can shift; you could get into a codependent relationship or a power game with your mentor. The mentor starts feeling his greatness and his power over you. When you come into your own power and say, "I don't want to give you that power anymore," you become the shadow of that mentor; he may get angry with you because you've taken your power back. Individuals who play these roles for you may not remain that way forever. They may shift according to the journey or the stage of the journey you are in. Once you complete a journey and start a new one, the same individuals may fill different roles. Some could play two different roles in your life simultaneously.

Remaining flexible and being able to dance and flow with these inner and outer forces is a critical capacity of Shakti Leadership.

ARCHETYPES SIMPLIFIED

All of this is terrific for script writing, but what relevance does it have for our lives? If you simplify these archetypes, you realize that they fall into two categories: those who are your enablers and those who are your disablers.

You only discover this after you've completed the journey, because while you're in it, the villain is the worst person in your life. But once you are done and you've learned your lessons and emerged with your elixir, you realize (as we said earlier) that no one is your enemy and no one is your friend; all alike are your teachers. Whether they're playing the role of enabler, which is one polarity, or of disabler, which is another polarity, they are helping create the energy field needed for you to cut through and find your power.

It is one thing to understand this. To live it, to cut through the polarities and unlock the energy — that is the journey.

THE DRAMA TRIANGLE

Most of us could certainly do with a little less drama in our lives! We often feel ill-treated and go running to someone else asking for their help, feeling like helpless victims of the situation.

How does drama get created? It is almost always because of another person who shows up in your life. By yourself, you may be perfectly fine and peaceful. But the minute a spouse, parent, daughter, or son enters your energy field and starts engaging with you, the two energy fields intersect. This intersection results in what physics calls *interference*, experienced by us as dissonance in our lives. The daily breakdown of equilibrium in human systems, at work or at home, is unavoidable. Depending on our personality type and orientation, we may experience it differently. But it will happen—that is a given. The name we give it and meaning we make of it can change.

This all comes together very nicely in a framework called the drama triangle, originated by Stephen Karpman.[5] It elegantly captures human dynamics and how we get into codependence with other people in our lives (Figure 6.3).

Something difficult happens in your life. You're really challenged, and you feel like a victim. When you enter this mode of victimhood, you automatically attract the opposite energy. You start projecting your victimhood onto someone: "I am a victim right now because of this person; he has done me wrong." When you get caught up in this persecutor/victim polarity, you will soon draw into your life a rescuer. Rescuers have an innate need to show up and help. They want to be needed and do good. People who become coaches and healers often take to these professions because they fit the archetype of rescuer.

For some time, the rescuer gives a lot of energy and the victim absorbs it happily but passively. The victim feels good because she's getting the support she needs, and the rescuer feels fabulous

Figure 6.3—*Drama Triangle*

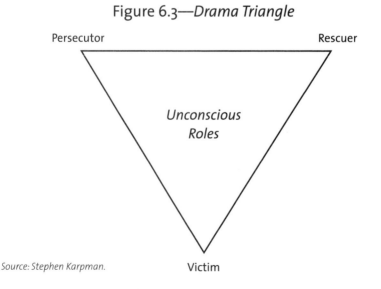

Persecutor   Rescuer

Unconscious Roles

Source: Stephen Karpman.   Victim

because she's needed. Then, inevitably, all the polarized energies swing. At some point, the rescuer starts to feel depleted, thinking, "No matter how much I give, it's never enough." The rescuer has become a victim, and the victim is now seen as a persecutor. Often, this is when the original persecutor starts showing up as a rescuer! The former rescuer starts understanding why the persecutor might have been behaving as they did. A strange kind of bond develops between them.

You enact this drama in your life in all your relationships where you are stuck in codependence with others. You're locked in this little dance of despair, depleting your energy in a downward spiral. This is what happens when we're unconsciously playing roles. Like a game of musical chairs, everyone shifts into a different mode but the drama continues.

How can we live differently? We have to wake up one day and realize that it is silly to continue playing this game. There is a better way, without all the drama.

Figure 6.4—*Drama to Dharma*

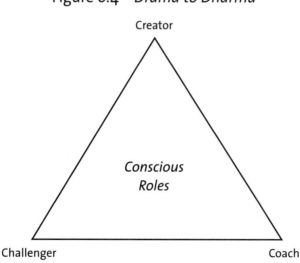

Creator

Conscious
Roles

Challenger   Coach

Derived from the book The Power of TED *by David Emerald, used with permission. www.powerofTED.com; www.consciousleadershipforum.com along with www.hendricks.com.*

From Drama to Dharma

Have hope! You are not in some endless dance of death with this other person. It takes just one person to change a situation, and that person is you. We learned from the work of Gay and Katie Hendricks that we can move from drama to dharma by flipping the triangle (Figure 6.4). When you start making these roles conscious, you start seeing them with more awareness. The first thing to do is to stop being a victim, and take on the role of a creator instead, by reframing the whole thing. Place yourself in a creator role and ask yourself how you can play with this dynamic. See the persecutor as a challenger, and seek help if you need it from a coach. Ask how both of these people can teach you and serve you: what can you learn from them?

Thinking of oneself as a victim of circumstances comes from a place of disempowerment. Step into the role of creator. If you were to take responsibility for your experience and how it is landing for you, what would you do? If the context is not okay for you, change it; do not accept the unacceptable. Take responsibility for the situation and your experience of it.

When you are the creator, see the persecutor as a challenger. Think about it: if you spar with someone stronger than yourself, or if you run alongside a pacer, they reveal your potential to you and help you attain it. They make you reconsider what you thought was your limit.

We often tell other people to change, but that rarely works. What does work is for you to shift internally, change your energy, start to carry your power and your weight on your own two feet, without leaning on someone or being overbearing. The minute you do that, the other person's energy has to shift. They cannot play the same game anymore because "it takes two to tango." Someone can be a perpetrator only if you are willing to be a victim. The minute you shift into creator energy, in which you are present and centered and carry your own weight, you change the energy of the other person.

Similarly, you can reframe your relationship with someone who is seeking to rescue you by holding your power as a creator and seeing them as your coach. You must run your own race, but you can take advantage of their support to raise your game. Use the challenger's energy to push you out of your comfort zone, and use the coach's energy to pull yourself up into a better place. The two roles can work in tandem to propel your growth in a healthy way.

The big shift is to move out of codependence into interdependence or even better, inter-independence. When you can lead yourself out of victimhood to become a creator, you can become your own rescuer. In a conscious way, you can be your own coach as well as challenger.

Assessing Your Leadership Style

It is very important to understand your dominant energy archetype. Some of us are more masculine in our leadership, others more feminine. It is fine to have a preference but it's important to recognize which is your dominant pole and which is your complementary pole.[6]

Shakti Leaders Speak: On Ground Leaders and Dynamic Leaders

Sally Kempton says,

Some leaders are ground leaders. They hold the space, and create a ground in which people can be creative. Some leaders are dynamic, in that they are like Steve Jobs, just endlessly creative Shaktis. At some basic level, leadership is about figuring out if you are a ground leader or a dynamic leader. The inner marriage is the ability to access both your static and dynamic states. My image of Shakti is the leopard who is completely still, the hunter who is totally unmoving but completely present until it unleashes its coiled power at the appropriate moment. This is the image of the Shiva/Shakti. The utter absolute patience of the stillness, which is not passive. It is coiled power waiting for its moment to act. In a state of presence, you hold both polarities. You know which one to play as needed. What may be initially a conscious act can become unconscious over time. You don't even need to know. You just naturally do.[7]

What do you focus on to get the job done? How do you exercise influence? How do you get others to do what is important? What energizes or drives you when working with others? How do you resolve disagreements or disputes? For each of these areas, there are multiple polarities, such as hierarchy (considered masculine) versus network (considered feminine), or level and status versus relationships (Figure 6.5). Fill in the appropriate score in each line, as it corresponds to you, to get a sense of what your style is (with –1 or +1 being least, and –3 or +3 being the most feminine or masculine, respectively). Sometimes you might be equally both, which means you put a '0' in the middle blank. There's no right or wrong way; it's just about becoming aware.

If you have scored a –3 or +3 on any front, ask yourself if there are situations where that may not be serving you. The takeaway from this exercise is that it's fine to have a dominant archetype, to be either masculine or feminine. But you must know this in order to call on the complementary energy when needed.

Former corporate executive Betty Ann Heggie uses a simple metaphor to explain how to balance our masculine and feminine energy in any situation as required. Think of hot and cold water from a tap. She says, "When you feel the water getting too hot, dial down the temperature by turning on the cold water tap. When it cools too much, turn the hot back on and reduce the cold until you find the perfect temperature."[8]

Pay particular attention to this when you find yourself in a leadership moment or dilemma and feeling stuck. You are stuck because what you're doing isn't working. That's when you need to know what to pull from the other pole. You can always use it, let it go when it's done, and come back to being in your anchored place.

Figure 6.5—*Masculine/Feminine Leadership Styles Assessment*

MASCULINE ←――――――――――――――――――→ FEMININE

1. Structure
(How you structure your team/work)

MASCULINE							FEMININE
Hierarchy	__	__	__	__	__	__	Network
Level and status matter	__	__	__	__	__	__	Relationships matter
Clear/separate roles	__	__	__	__	__	__	Overlapping roles
Top down power/info	__	__	__	__	__	__	Power/info shared

2. Orientation
(What do you focus on to get the job done)

Goal/result	__	__	__	__	__	__	Process
Push aside distracting ideas	__	__	__	__	__	__	Gather multiple inputs, weigh related issues

3. Influence
(How you get others to do what is important to you)

Command	__	__	__	__	__	__	Persuade
Give orders/tell	__	__	__	__	__	__	Make requests/ask
Direct/clear	__	__	__	__	__	__	Indirect/polite
Appeal to logic/prove	__	__	__	__	__	__	Appeal to emotion/inspire

4. Motivation
(What energizes or drives you when working with others)

Competition	__	__	__	__	__	__	Collaboration
Work is a game to be won	__	__	__	__	__	__	Opp to co-create/belong
Coming out on top is key	__	__	__	__	__	__	Involving team and sharing power is key

5. Conflict
(How you resolve disagreements and disputes)

Confront directly	__	__	__	__	__	__	Approach indirectly
Facts have priority	__	__	__	__	__	__	Feelings and facts imp.
Seek closure	__	__	__	__	__	__	Seek healing
Transactional (don't take personally)	__	__	__	__	__	__	Emotional (go through hurt/pain)

+3 +2 +1 0 −1 −2 −3

Total your +Masculine score and −Feminine score. Depending on which one is higher, you're leading more from that energy.

Think of a dilemma you are facing.
1. Which of the above five domains is it about?
2. What style or energy (M/F) do you need to dial up or down?

Adapted from Caroline Turner, "A Balance of Both Masculine and Feminine Strengths: The Bottom-Line Benefit," Forbes, May 7, 2012. www.forbes.com/sites/womensmedia/2012/05/07/a-balance-of-both-masculine-and-feminine-strengths-the-bottom-line-benefit/.[9]

The whole idea of flexibility is that you should be anchored in yourself, but also know how to flex toward something else. Bend, but don't break. Bend toward it and then come right back when you no longer need it.

Remember that the ideal to strive for is the *ardhanarishwar*, the beautiful depiction of half man–half woman in the yogic tradition: to have transcended gender and its surface qualities. Learn to hold both and play to one or the other as needed.

Avivah Wittenberg-Cox is a consultant who helps to build gender-balanced businesses. She advocates that businesses and their employees learn to be "gender-bilingual"—to speak the language of the feminine as well as the language of the masculine.[10] Speak the language of the country you are in. But you don't stop being the other.

Cultivating Positive Masculine and Feminine Traits

Once we understand that choosing only our masculine or feminine nature is as unsustainable as choosing only to inhale or to exhale, the next question is: *how* do we cultivate our necessary complementary qualities?

There is a simple answer: just the same as we *learn* any skill.

- We identify what we want to cultivate. Let's take the quality of gentleness.

- Take it up as a quality you want to genuinely learn. Adopt it as your leadership practice or *sadhana* for the week. Write it up as a big sticker on your preferred screen/s: "Gentleness."

- Start paying attention to this quality and apply it intentionally in your leadership moments and relationships over the next week or so. Note the outcome.

- Identify some role models who exemplify this quality and study how they do it.

- Watch YouTube videos or enroll in a life-skills/soft-skills class that teaches this. For example, a simple 5 to 10 minute Buddhist meditation called *metta* practice leads you to embodying loving kindness or gentleness. We have shared it with you as part of the higher-self dialogue on page 122.

- Try it on for size. Practice it relentlessly. If necessary begin with low-risk situations. Much like riding a cycle, you may be awkward at first. But with committed practice, you will find that you have gone from unconscious incompetence to conscious incompetence, then to conscious competence, and finally to unconscious competence that comes quite naturally.[11]

- Once you've mastered the quality to a degree of satisfaction, take up the next quality you wish to develop.

All these qualities are potentially within you. You have to have the heroic heart to make the effort and find the teacher—if needed, to fake it 'til you make it. Your cause is worthy, so don't worry about falling and failing a few times.

If failing is a fear, then the next quality you may wish to take up is vulnerability.

Our advice may sound simple, but it comes from some of the world's great wisdom traditions. For example, monks in Buddhist training are told to take up a higher emotion such as compassion, loving kindness, empathy, or equanimity as their daily practice and are tested by their teachers accordingly. Much like going to a gym is an effective way to build our biceps, taking up such a routine is effective in building our masculine/feminine traits.

Practices for Integrating Masculine and Feminine

Michael Gelb recommends the following practices to help integrate our masculine and feminine natures:

- Cultivate patience, receptivity, and empathetic listening.
- Be bold and assertive when appropriate.

- Learn to move freely from patience and receptivity to bold action and vice versa.

- Balance imagination and logic, intuition and analysis. Use your whole brain.

- Cultivate the "ability to behave with compassion and wisdom while maintaining inner and outer peace regardless of the circumstances."[12]

- Transform stress with the Love Response—teach yourself how to shift from a fear state to a love state.[13]

- Be aware of your anxiety and do not be afraid to deeply feel your feelings. (This may be the single most important thing.)

- Embrace a daily practice to facilitate the integration of masculine and feminine energies. Do *pranayama* (regulating the breath through various techniques), Tai Chi, or some other practice every single day to help change your nervous system, to be more aligned and attuned to this new integration.

Conscious leaders are flexible. They know how to draw Shakti from all the different forces available and use each as needed; they are not fixated on any one way of being or doing things. They adapt, unlearn, and learn with agility, leveraging all polarities with presence, coming unstuck from all *ors* and finding the best in all *ands*.

In the next chapter, we look at a third important capacity of Shakti Leadership: achieving congruence.

7

ACHIEVING CONGRUENCE

The third capacity of conscious leadership that comes out of presence and true power is congruence. As we traverse life's path, existential concerns can pervade our mind, leaving us with a fragile sense of purpose and unanswered questions such as "Who am I? Where have I come from? Where am I going? How will I get there?"

This chapter will unfold the placard of I AM – I CAN – I WILL: a mantra that will help every leader know their story and discover their personal myth. It will help them divine their *swadharma*—a commitment to themselves and their objective of fully manifesting their Shakti in selfless service and fulfillment of their highest purpose.

A CONSCIOUS LEADER IS CONGRUENT

We define congruence as the capacity to be centered, authentic, and aligned with one's purpose both internally (how one feels) and externally (how one acts). Recall that getting to wholeness was about "stepping in" to gather all the fragmented parts of yourself. The next capacity, flexibility, was about "stepping up" as a leader who proactively shapes and engages with life rather than just reacting to it. Congruence is about "stepping out," venturing out into the world to be of service in a way that is uniquely yours. Conscious leaders know what their purpose is, they know their story, they know where they came from, and they know where they are going. They are living their *swadharma*—their unique personal calling.

Dharma means righteous action. *Swadharma* means right actions that are unique to each individual, according to their own innate nature, their *swabhav*. *Swadharma* is that sweet spot where our work and love come together in a completely satisfying way, setting us free even as it fulfills us. No two people can have the same *swadharma*; you can't live someone else's *swadharma* for them. Your *swabhav* (innate nature) shapes your *swadharma*. The texture and nature of your *swabhav* determines the direction from which you will flow. You must be congruent internally according to your *swabhav*, instead of futilely struggling to be a square peg in a round hole. And you should be congruent externally toward your *swadharma*.

Shakti Leaders are audaciously ambitious but not for themselves. "It's not about building bigger companies but about serving something bigger," says John Gerzema, co-author of *The Athena Doctrine*. "There's so much cynicism that people are out for short-term gain. Leadership today is about taking people into a better future. That's a long trip."[1]

Casey Sheahan, former CEO of Patagonia, is a leader who is deeply aligned with his higher purpose. But that purpose isn't self-centered. As he says, "Running a business with a higher purpose, such as Whole Foods or Patagonia, taps into creative energy, creative consciousness. Running a business that way generally gives you great success, but it's not your real reason for being; your reason is to elevate mankind, to be able to live a better life and be happier."[2]

Shakti Leaders Speak: On Ambition

Gerry Laybourne, co-founder, former chairman and CEO of Oxygen Media, recalls:

I remember one instance where a person who was working directly for me came to me and said, "Do you want to be a vice president?" My response was "I couldn't care less. I want to make something great for kids. That's what I am focused on." She said, "If you have so little ambition, I'm going to get another job." I said, "You should do that." I have plenty of ambition, but it's not a self-centered ambition. It's an ambition to actually change something. That was just unthinkable to her.[3]

PURPOSE ↔ *SWADHARMA* ↔ PLEASURE!

A profound insight from yogic wisdom is that living your purpose, your *swadharma*, is also the source of your *ananda*, your deepest pleasure or bliss. Your purpose is not some dull, onerous, or scary thing that you have to do; it's not simply a duty. It is in fact your greatest pleasure. When you have discovered your dharma, you have found the way to your bliss. You can live it day in and day out and it will continually energize you instead of depleting you.

Traditional work, something that's "just a job," depletes you, because you're using up your limited store of energy. But when you're grounded in your *swabhav* and working from there, it's as if you're constantly plugged into an inexhaustible source of energy. You just have to live; the more you work and live your dharma, the more energized you feel.

Clues for Discerning Your *Swabhav* and *Swadharma*

The Enneagram is a well-known personality typing system. According to *The Wisdom of the Enneagram*, you may be carrying one (or more) of these innate gifts.[4]

Speak these affirmations out aloud and see which resonates the most for you.

1. I live for a higher purpose.

2. I nurture myself and others.

3. I raise the benchmark and set an example.

4. I create and renew myself constantly.

5. I bring clarity and insight without judgment or expectation.

6. I believe in myself and trust others.

7. I celebrate joyously and share happiness.

8. I stand up, speak out, and act with courage.

9. I bring healing and harmony to the world.

Shakti is present in each of these ways of being and doing, as they are all capacities that come from one's core, authentic presence.

Once you know what innate power you can draw from, sense your *swadharma* as bringing your *swabhav* to bear upon one of the three domains of higher human pursuit:

The Good: Doing what is right for the world

The True: Pursuit and expansion of human knowledge

The Beautiful: Excellence and the creation of beauty

These are called the Platonic ideals, each a worthy end in itself; Aristotle called them "goods of first intent." There is a fair chance that where your innate true nature (one of the nine Ennea-gifts) meets its domain of ideal action (the Good, True, and/or Beautiful) lies your *swadharma*, a personal higher purpose with which you are congruent.

Nilima shares that she found her congruence when she came to the work of empowering women and gender reconciliation by bringing yogic wisdom (consciousness and Shakti) in service of creating a world that works for all. From her core, she resonates with the first gift of the Enneagram (living for a higher purpose) and is inspired to bring it to doing Good (what's right for the world). Shakti Leadership is the outcome of this quest and rings true for her, even as she is occasionally tested and stretched into living it more fully in all aspects of her life, including keeping a sense of humor, lightening up, and embracing her "foolish" self!

Raj discovered a quality in himself of learning to trust his own instincts and judgment and innately trusting others (the sixth gift of the Enneagram). He was inspired to use his academic training to pursue the truth about whether the conscious way of being can actually succeed in the world, especially in the dog-eat-dog world of business. This gave rise to his book *Firms of Endearment*, which showed that companies built on trust and caring can be enormously successful in the world if they also have a deep sense of purpose, seek to serve rather than use all their stakeholders, and elevate leaders who care about people and purpose ahead of power and personal enrichment. This work was foundational to the launch of the global Conscious Capitalism movement.

We have all experienced moments when we felt we were really in our element and completely alive. That is us living our dharma. Dharma isn't necessarily about taking up a specific profession or career. It's more about who you are and how you show up in the world—what you are meant to manifest. The energy with which you do it and the energy you bring into the world ring true. That is what it means to live the dharmic life.

Most companies refer to their people as "human resources." But think about what that implies. Most resources are limited and get depleted with use. A lump of coal is a resource; once you use it, it burns out. Human beings are indeed subject to burnout when they are treated like resources, when they are not connected to a living, vibrant source. But a human being who is in a supportive setting and operating in harmony with her *swabhav* and *swadharma* is an inexhaustible fountain of energy, caring, creativity, and compassion. You go from being a depleted *resource* to a limitless *source*, because you are plugged into the infinitely powerful and creative ultimate source, Shakti.[5]

What is the meaningful purpose of life? What are we here to do and be? The ancient texts of India speak of *purushartha*, which literally means the "object of human pursuit." The *purushartha* cites four goals or aims of a human life: *dharma*, *artha*, *kama*, and *moksha*. Dharma is about our duties and the right way to live.

Artha is about prosperity and the means of life, but also about purpose and meaning. That's the masculine part of us. *Kama* is about pleasure, love, and relationships (our feminine side), and *moksha* is about liberation and self-realization. The sweet spot where dharma, *artha*, and *kama* come together is where your *swadharma* is (Figure 7.1). You don't have to choose one over the other; you can live all of them, and that defines the seat of your pleasure. From this arises a portal to *moksha*, liberation, the great freedom and joy beyond duality.

At the end of all his work, Joseph Campbell brought it down to these three words: "Follow your bliss." Life is *ananda* (bliss). It is born out of *ananda*, it exists and sustains in *ananda*, and it returns to *ananda*. *The Age of Ananda* author Kumar Sharma advises us to "Live joyously and evolve consciously." It takes deep inner work and maturation to come into one's bliss. Until then, as Andrew

Figure 7.1—*Purpose* ↔ Swadharma ↔ *Pleasure!*

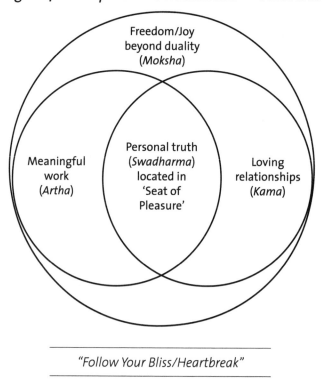

Freedom/Joy
beyond duality
(*Moksha*)

Meaningful
work
(*Artha*)

Personal truth
(*Swadharma*)
located in
'Seat of
Pleasure'

Loving
relationships
(*Kama*)

"Follow Your Bliss/Heartbreak"

Harvey says, "Follow your heartbreak." What is it in the world that causes you deep, almost physical anguish—something that you feel urgently needs tending to, healing, or setting right? This may well point to your *swadharma*, your unique purpose to follow and fulfill. This heartbreak may be your "call to adventure," which, once heeded, will lead you to the elixir and to your bliss.

We all feel heartache at the conflict and destruction around us, from the personal to planetary levels. All we can do is acknowledge the heartbreak, offer it to our higher self, and wait for inner guidance on what loving action that self needs from us.

A time comes when bliss and heartbreak mysteriously connect. When heartbreak feels like bliss and bliss like heartbreak, this is what holding the whole feels like—sweet and sharp at the same time, the *ananda* that is beyond bliss and heartbreak. This is *mahakaruna*—profound and utter compassion for the human condition, an irresistible impulse that galvanizes us to healing action.

MANIFESTING YOUR HIGHER PURPOSE

What is your bliss and how can you get in touch with it? Once you know who you are and what your *swadharma* is, you can claim it and commit to it. You become a blissful and unstoppable force of nature. Other people's business will no longer matter, because you will be so consumed with your own—in a healthy way, of course!

How can you find that "red thread"? Take an inventory of all the things you have done in your life, especially those that you most enjoyed. They may seem on the surface to be fairly divergent and different. But can you detect a recurring pattern through them all? If you can find it, that red thread will give you a clue to what is really your gift and thus your path.

You can also use a more structured approach to discover your higher purpose (Figure 7.2). When you move forward into this grand new life, you don't completely discard the past. Start by looking at the knowledge and skills you have gained through your education, training, and life experiences. For most people, it's no

Figure 7.2—*Higher Purpose*

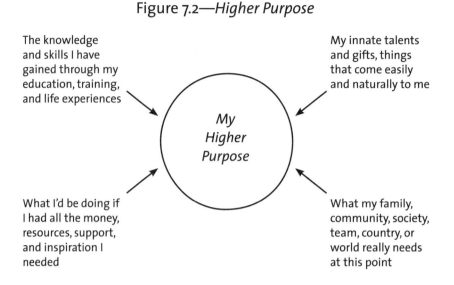

The knowledge and skills I have gained through my education, training, and life experiences

My innate talents and gifts, things that come easily and naturally to me

My Higher Purpose

What I'd be doing if I had all the money, resources, support, and inspiration I needed

What my family, community, society, team, country, or world really needs at this point

accident that they've been educated in a particular subject instead of something else. The core of what you've already learned can serve as a building block.

Next, consider your innate talents and gifts, those things that come easily and naturally to you. Maybe you could always sing or write effortlessly, or whatever you cook is delicious, or you just know how to make people feel comfortable. There's something about you that works very naturally and has always been there. Author Gay Hendricks in his book *The Big Leap* refers to this as your "Zone of Genius."

Now think about what you would be doing if you had all the money, resources, support, and inspiration that you needed. If you didn't have to meet any of your duties first, what would you do with your life?

Finally, look at the world and ask, "What are the gaps out there? What does my family, community, society, team, country, or the world really need at this point?" Innately, each of us has a desire to do something positive in the world—something worth pursuing for its own sake. The gap could be big or small evoking a vivid sense that "someone needs to do something about that." That someone may well be you. As John Donne wrote (and Ernest Hemingway made famous), " . . . never send to know for whom the bell tolls; it tolls for thee."

Your unique higher purpose is very likely to be found at the intersection of these four things.

Shakti Leaders Speak: On Finding Purpose

Casey Sheahan, former CEO of Patagonia, quested for years to discover his purpose:

I made many trips to India and met with many beautiful teachers, some of whom spent time with me in my home in Colorado. I was looking at how I was showing up in the world personally, knowing that any suffering that I had in me connected to my self-centricity and would have an effect on others. I did this work to become aware of that so I could diminish my ego and become a different kind of leader who would be a powerful fit for the culture at Patagonia. I created a higher vision for my life, starting with myself and my family and then my employees and my company, to help make our communities and the world a better place. It started with looking at my own emotions and ideas and actions and being aware when I was doing things out of self-interest or ambition, which is very common with a leader of a company because you fall into patterns where if you have a big job or you're successful, you think it's all about you.

I loved my job at Patagonia because I would leap up the stairs two at a time every morning to see what business adventure awaited me. If you have the right vision for your life and for your work and stay true to yourself, then you know what you're doing every day when you wake up. It has nothing to do with the twenty things on your to-do list; it's just how you show up and how you're going to impact others. If it is in accordance with conscious leadership, it's how you're going to help others realize their full potential and be the most incredible happy human beings that they can be. The role can be all about you as the hero, or it can be about supporting every other human being on the planet. That was what happened to me coming out of my four trips to India. It made me enjoy life even more and I had great success with my business as well.[6]

DIALOGUE WITH THE HIGHER SELF

The "higher-self dialogue" is a practice that can help you discover your purpose. It assumes that we each have an ego self, rooted in our ordinary mind, and also a higher self—a divinized version of our self—that understands our essence better than our ego self does and can guide and protect us at all times. It knows that which we truly seek.

Since we are frequently told not to aggrandize the ordinary ego self, we run the risk of throwing the baby out with the bathwater by neglecting to honor our higher self. The more you are in touch with the higher self—the more you acknowledge and honor it—the more you can step into your own power and authenticity.

Inner growth is all about developing a relationship with this higher self. One way to do so is to stop and give thanks to that self every time you sense its power and presence and support. As you journey through challenges and ordeals, you will slowly come to experience your higher self as your powerful invisible partner.

The higher-self dialogue to discern one's higher purpose is a deep meditation and exploration drawing from many different psycho-spiritual and creative processes, including Buddhist *metta* practice, Integral Yoga, psychosynthesis, inner-child work, and creative visualization. It aims to bypass the rational mind and access the consciousness of all parts of our being, especially the creative child and the empathic and wise higher self. It has three steps.

Step 1: Opening the Heart and Embracing the Inner Child

Start by creating a sacred space for yourself. Sit down in a chair and place both feet firmly on the ground. Keep your back straight and eyes closed. Enter into the awareness of your everyday "here

and now" ordinary self. To start opening your heart and chan-
neling your presence, bring into your mind's eye your child-self.
Recall when that child-self first encountered some kind of fear
or insecurity, felt foolish or lost. See this child-self in front of
you very clearly. As a parent would, gently and lovingly hold
your child-self, your right hand on the child's left shoulder, and
your left hand around the right waist. Enter into communion with
your precious child-self. Send deep *metta* (loving kindness) to this
child-self. Say to the child, "May you be well; may you be happy;
may you be free from all suffering."

Keep breathing and integrating the energy of this child-self
with your adult-self. Try to reconnect with your childlike curios-
ity and joy to open your heart and mind to a sense of adventure
and playfulness. Breathe healing into your child-self and receive
wonder and playfulness in return. From this place of integration
of your adult-self and child-self, bring heightened awareness to
that sense of joy or bliss that you had when you were a child and
that you still carry as an adult. Articulate any question you might
have of life right now, such as trying to understand your choices,
discern your red thread, resolve your dilemmas, determine what
to do and what not to do.

Bring all that into your awareness and consideration now
from this place of integration.

Take a piece of paper and fill in the four quadrants shown in
Figure 7.2. Write down the knowledge and skills that you have
gained through your education and training. Capture your innate
talents and gifts, things that come naturally to you. Imagine what
you'd be doing if you had all the money and time and support in
the world. Sense what the world needs, what your team needs,
or life itself needs.

If you could ask an all-knowing being a question, what would
it be? Articulate with great clarity and specificity this deep and
central question: *What is my purpose?*

Step 2: Opening the Mind and Accessing the Higher Self

When you have fully and clearly articulated the central question of your higher purpose, stand up very slowly and come around your chair, facing its back. Imagine your ego self sitting in front of you. Keeping your eyes closed, drop your hands. Hold the integrity of the energy. Place your feet shoulder-width apart and make yourself tall. You're a powerful, mighty, immovable mountain now. You have relocated yourself into the consciousness of your higher self, the all-knowing, all-powerful being that you are. Embody that energy now. Call upon it, feel it enter you and open to it. Very gently place your hands on the back of the chair as if you're placing them on the shoulders of your ego self below. With great compassion and understanding, allow your higher self to channel your own highest power and wisdom. It's as though you've opened a tap and let the stream of consciousness flow. Let the words come. Be a silent, receptive container. Let the wisdom flow through you, wisdom that is for the highest good of all. Once you feel the tap has opened and the stream of consciousness has started flowing, gently sit down and start writing. Write everything that comes to you. Allow clarity to emerge on its own. Don't direct with your mind; let your intuition take over. Start integrating and absorbing it into your being. If it comes together as one phrase or statement, write that in the central box of Figure 7.2.

Step 3: Integrating and Accepting Your Power Symbol and Personal Myth

Once you are done writing, close your eyes again and relax. Imagine that you're walking in a beautiful forest and the weather is perfect; it's a bright, sunny day, the birds are chirping in the skies. There's a wonderful fragrance in the air. You're walking down a trail. There's an unmistakable sense that something magical, something very powerful and sublime awaits you. As you walk, the bushes get thicker, but you continue, undeterred. Your will sharpens, and your commitment and resolve are strengthened to go and meet whatever it is that awaits you. You have a smile on your face, feeling a sense of anticipation and of joy.

Find yourself stepping into a clearing, with dappled sunlight around you. In the middle of this cleared space is a mirror with a veil over it. It feels like a very sacred, holy space. Take off your footwear and wash your hands and face in the clean running stream nearby. Your truest, purest self steps forward now and moves toward that mirror and invites you to lift that veil. Take a deep breath, remove the veil from the mirror, and allow yourself to gaze into the vast innerscape the mirror is showing you. Approaching you from the other side, through the mirror, is a symbol, someone or something, which you come to recognize as the unique symbol of your power. "This is me. The power that is me is being shown to me through this symbol." The most powerful, beautiful energy radiates out of this object or being. All you have to do is reach out and be open to it and breathe, and it comes into you and merges with you. It's as if you've been switched on, have come alive. Your whole body is singing and smiling because you know the energy deep inside every cell of your body right now is saying, "I am this, I am this, I am this."

Such is the beauty of this reconnection with your power that you want to capture it in a poster that you can take back with you. Every time you forget who you are, you just have to check this poster. When you're ready, create the poster of your power symbol. It's not about producing an artistic drawing; it's about capturing the essence of what you felt. Draw something that captures the pleasure and the power of who you are when you're in your element. Invite your right brain to come forth. The symbol should appeal to not just your heart, your head, or your gut, but to all three.

Having tuned in to your intuition, from a place of presence (especially a calm mind) and complete honesty, do a reality check. Does your higher purpose ring clear and true to you? Don't force-fit it. Reword it until it does. Does it appeal to your head, heart, and gut? Does it fit you and stretch you at the same time? You need the right balance of comfort and discomfort, because without discomfort you cannot grow! Does it compel you to act? Is there the fierce energy of Shakti about it? If there is, it will energize and motivate you for years to come, until it finds fulfillment.

I Am. I Can. I Will.

Claim your personal conscious leadership myth. First, consider:

My presence: How will I cultivate it?

My power: How will I exercise it?

My pleasure: How will I find it?

My purpose: How will I live it?

Then tell your unique story in the third person: Who is s/he? What is the unique gift that empowers her/him? Where is s/he going? What is the higher purpose that energizes her/him? What's getting in her/his way? What obstacles does s/he need to overcome? How will s/he get there? What resources can s/he draw upon?

Dialoging with your higher self and articulating your personal myth are ongoing, iterative, and evolving processes. Feel free to play with our suggested processes and find your own way.

Organizational Higher-Self Dialogue

If you were able to get in touch with a sense of the gift you embody, the purpose that you are here to bring to the world, you can also bring this process and approach to an organization you are part of. It could be very old or a recent startup. Organizations are on their own heroic journey and go through the same cycle that we as individuals go through. Just as we have articulated a higher purpose for who we are and where we are going, the organization should articulate its higher purpose. Not many organizations have the ability to discern the soul of their being, and so their purpose statements feel empty and unrelatable; these organizations are a shell without a soul. But if the right people with the right tools and skills come together and craft that statement, it becomes an inspiring call and a galvanizing force.

TOWARD SELF-MASTERY AND SELFLESS SERVICE

The heroic journey includes parallel inner and outer journeys in the ultimate quest for freedom and fulfillment. The outer track is your journey through leadership, and the inner track is the journey of the evolution of your consciousness. The two occur simultaneously. The leader you become is the person you become.

OUTER JOURNEY	INNER JOURNEY
• Achieve tasks	• Achieve growth
• Overcome obstacles	• Overcome neuroses
• Heal relationships	• Heal inner schisms
• From innocent to leader	• From victim to creator
• Raise collective consciousness	• Raise own consciousness
• Uplift society	• Evolve self
LEADS TO SELFLESS SERVICE	**LEADS TO SELF MASTERY**

Freedom to Live; Master of Two Worlds

The outer journey is where tasks are achieved and obstacles overcome. We heal some relationships that may have been broken. We go from being the untested innocent to the leader of that space, and we raise the collective consciousness of our tribe, our communities, our teams, our societies. In the process, society gets uplifted.

On the inner journey, you achieve personal growth. You overcome your neuroses and heal the schisms and splits inside you.

You go from being a victim to becoming a creator. You raise your consciousness and evolve your self.

When you journey on the outside you arrive at a place of self-less service to the world and to your higher purpose. The journey inside brings you to a place of self-mastery. They're two sides of the same coin, mutually enhancing and interdependent capacities. The more self-mastery you can achieve, the more you can go out and accomplish great things. The more you are in service, the more mastery you build. Each mirrors and parallels the other. The outer journey is about *doing*; the inner journey about *being*. When you become the master of your self, you're no longer egoic or power-based; instead, you're in complete selfless service to your tribe, your community, your purpose, whatever that higher ideal may be. Riding the waves of change, both inner and outer, helps you become a "master of two worlds," in Campbell's phrase. It is the state from which you can finally experience the full freedom to live. Having overcome your conditioning and reclaimed your power from all the archetypes that were driving your psychological car, you are now truly free, fully in charge.

At journey's end, the world will see you as the innocent who has come into your own as a leader. You, on the other hand, have reframed your powerlessness and evolved yourself into a potent new creator-being, with a welcome ability to laugh at yourself—a wise-fool at ease with tough-love. This is the sweet-spot of holding lightly one's eros-thanatos-logos-mythos!

Shakti Leaders Speak: On Higher Purpose

When it comes to higher purpose, Casey Sheahan asks,

At some point, is everything all about yourself? Are you running a business just so you're successful? Or are you thinking about the growth of all your stakeholders—their lives, their happiness, their fulfillment? Operating from the ambitious side of the page is all about aggression and self-centricity. Just think what kind of example you are setting for your children and your organization if you're operating from that side of the page. If this is the culture of the organization, what's the future? If your people aren't happy, do you really think you're going to be successful? The other side of the equation is living life with a spiritual vision—with compassion, love, and understanding. This has to begin with a vision for yourself to get to a higher inner state of being—feel good about how you're living your life and how you're conducting your business and helping all the people in your organization become free of suffering. On the ambition side of the equation, suffering is behind the fear and greed, the "make money at all costs" mindset, the comparisons with other people's success … all those notions are really about creating you as separate from other individuals, because you're trying to create an organization or business that is better than the others, makes more money, "I'm richer, I'm the best," etc.[7]

We're all journeying toward our freedom or *ananda*, our bliss. We only attain that when we master both the worlds: the inner as well as the outer. This is the great elixir, the final outcome of why we journey, and it's why we have no choice *but* to journey.

8

THE PROMISE OF SHAKTI LEADERSHIP: A FULFILLED AND FREE WORLD

If there is to be a future,
it will wear a crown of feminine design.

Sri Aurobindo[1]

THE ELEPHANT IN THE ROOM

We came across a *New Yorker* cartoon recently that shows a depressed elephant lying on its psychotherapist's couch, saying, "I'm right there in the room, and no one even acknowledges me."

That elephant in the room reminded us of Shakti, the unseen, unacknowledged, and unused feminine power. Elephants symbolize gentleness, intelligence, and great strength—a fitting symbol for Shakti.

The power and even the existence of Shakti has long been staunchly denied, perhaps because it has been seen as a threat to society's traditionally patriarchal structures. Those holding the reins of power have long sensed and perhaps secretly feared this potently feminine power of life in women. Thus they have sought to keep it harnessed and tied down to serve their patriarchal systems. To prevent this power from manifesting its greatness, we have acquiesced to a collective amnesia; we have chosen to implicitly accept the canard that feminine qualities are inferior to masculine ones. Thus the patriarchy has been and continues to be enabled to feel in near-total control of the uncertain processes of life and destiny.

The win-lose consciousness of an immature humanity has caused us to deny, suppress, and devalue the power and indispensability of the feminine in order to maintain the dominance of the masculine. We have so lost sight and sense of Shakti's existence that we struggle even now to bring it into our awareness, to observe and understand what Shakti really is.

Human history has been filled with great scientific, artistic, and material advances, but also with unimaginable suffering—of one pointless war after another, each sowing the seeds of the next eruption of violence, in an endless succession of acts of manly bravado, unleavened by the nourishing, humanizing, and civilizing touch of the mature feminine. Countless precious, unique, and irreplaceable human lives have been tragically cut short, and all for what? To appease the egos and quench the blood lust of tyrants and despots, and not much else.

Ego-based power and money have long been seen as "the only games in town." It is time to awaken to the enlivening reality that there are much bigger, better, and more fulfilling games in town. We interviewed many leaders and leadership experts for this book. What struck us was that most of the necessary behaviors, skills, and attitudes they called for and highlighted as essential to human flourishing are at their core fundamentally feminine—that is, aspects of Shakti. In many cases, people are not even aware that these are feminine elements. This is why Shakti feels like the invisible elephant in the room. How can we miss seeing the very principle that hold up life?

Such is the extent of submersion of the feminine in our individual and collective unconscious that we have to dive deep to retrieve it and reengage with it. This creative and sustaining feminine power is intelligent and conscious. It is real and powerful beyond the comprehension of most. The sooner we recognize what belongs to the domain of the feminine, the more conscious we can become of its agency. The more we learn to work with it, the more effective and fulfilled we will become.

Recent research on leadership has unearthed many desirable qualities that are inherently gifts of Shakti. It is like the well-known parable of the blind men describing different parts of the same elephant. Rather than grasping for pieces of the puzzle, we are better served by trying to understand the whole.

Earlier, we wrote of how baby elephants are conditioned into domestic labor by being chained to a tree. They do not know their own strength as they grow up and are seemingly content to remain in the confines of the same space, even as they grow into their immense power and the chain around their foot is unshackled from the tree. The time has finally come for feminine energy to break out of the conditioning it has been under for many millennia and realize it has the power to move mountains—in both men and women, and in the world. It is time, at long last, to finally unshackle Shakti and celebrate its power and grace and bountiful gifts.

Shakti Leaders Speak: On Living Your Life and Values

Shelly Lazarus, chairman of Ogilvy & Mather Worldwide, advises:

You cannot be afraid to be who you are. Live your values, live your life. I heard a woman the other day use the term "sneaking out of the office" to go to her child's play. That's how she described her own behavior. I said, "Wait! Stop right there. I have never snuck out of any place; I walk right down the center hall, and if anybody doesn't like it, too bad! This is what I need to do to lead my life, this is what I want to do. I'm going to the school play—at 11:15 A.M. Don't worry about me, I will get my job done. I will deliver whatever people need. But don't sneak. Just stand up, do what you need to do and smile about it, and look 'em in the eye and say 'If you don't like it, fire me! I'll go find another job, because I'm talented enough and I'm committed enough and I'm smart enough.'"[2]

SHAKTI'S JOURNEY

We are in the early stages of awakening to the realization that the path we have been on for millennia is not working anymore, and indeed never really worked in the past either. It is not working in our individual lives, as evidenced by the epidemics of depression, addiction, and chronic disease we are suffering in growing numbers.[3] It is also not working at a collective, planetary level; witness the degradation of the environment and the destruction of countless species.

We are approaching a monumental societal tipping point. A fast-growing number of men are starting to become comfortable integrating the feminine side into their approach to life and leadership. At the same time, huge numbers of women are coming through the education system, rising through organizational hierarchies and assuming leadership roles. With those rising numbers comes greater confidence in their own capacities; women are no longer in a world in which they feel they must emulate the most egregious aspects of masculine behavior in order to succeed.

When you lead with Shakti, you're tapping into the power that fuels the universe: the power of love and care and mutuality. You're not operating at cross-purposes with where the world needs to and wants to go. You're an agent of something that is essentially infinite. You become part of Shakti's own journey, the general rise of the feminine in the world.

Even as we start by seeing ourselves as the hero/ine of our life's story, a time comes when we have to become a part of a larger journey, when our small stream merges into the mighty river of Shakti herself. Chris Maddox, founder of The Wild Woman Project, summarizes it thus: "This is (the) shift: from feeling like the star of the movie of my life with a really pretty set, to feeling like part of an epic story being told where I am honored to have a tiny, yet mighty role in this chapter."[4]

The narrative of Conscious Leadership is incomplete without unveiling and making explicit the idea of Shakti, the power that activates consciousness and embodies the full spectrum of energies that fuel and mediate our evolution. Making this power, this dynamic energy field, discernible and getting acquainted with the archetypes/drives at work within and around us, is critical to our growth. We cannot come into any level of mastery—personal, professional, or collective—until we become aware of and consciously work with these invisible forces.

Author Caroline Myss refers to this Shakti energy in her own language: "Our interior nature is evolving to accommodate the energetic age in which we now reside. Our intuitive intelligence has awakened along with other inner senses causing all sorts of disruptions. . . . Yet we are not familiar with the subtleties of our psychic and indeed our spiritual intelligence. We now truly reside as much in the invisible realm of the psyche and the energy world (via technology) as we do in the physical world. . . . I believe that it is equally important to learn to speak 'archetypes' fluently because symbols and myths are the language of the psyche."[5]

EVERYTHING JOURNEYS

Many readers will remember playing the game Mastermind as children, a game in which we had to crack a hidden code. With each step we took, we got closer to discerning what it was.

The code of life is that, in order to come into being, *everything journeys*.

Ideas, movements, institutions, and programs are tested, just as species, communities, and individuals are. Only those that are "fit to survive" endure and thrive. For example, the path from the Declaration of Independence to the establishment of a stable democratic system of government in the United States was a difficult and treacherous one. The young country's leaders had to overcome numerous challenges and deal with circumstances that could have killed the fledgling nation before it was able to find its true identity. The journey of growth and evolution continues to this day and will never end.

The journey has an astonishingly intelligent design built in to it. By now, thanks to Joseph Campbell's work, the stages and archetypal characters are well known. With fresh eyes and full presence, you can anticipate the stages of the journey and respond consciously. Just as you can use the ordeals to come into your own power and Shakti rather than being consumed by them, you can do the same for any organization or movement that you are part of or care about.

The inner journey to self-mastery is as important as the outer journey to selfless service. Don't lose track of one for the other. You're not just here to wake up and fulfill your personal agenda. Your personal hero's journey is linked to your company's success, societal renaissance, and global harmony. You're here to find your *swadharma* and follow your bliss and in doing so play your part in the grand symphony of evolutionary growth.

Sri Aurobindo's "Human Cycle" describes the inevitability of our impending evolution. He says that we're not just doing *sadhana* and practice for our own self-development and our own freedom and perfection, the reasons most people usually do any spiritual practice. The time has come for us to know the context of *why* we are doing it: to support evolution itself. This whole creation is a work in progress. Only when a critical mass of people wake up is anything going to shift. We're still caught in the old context, and that context is slow to change, which means we get stuck and pulled back all the time. We need to bring additional intentionality into the spiritual practices we undergo, the intention that what we are doing is to further evolution itself, to further creation, and to further humanity. It is not a selfish purpose; it is the highest act of selflessness. That is why we must make our heroic journey at this time.

You have a broad sense of the destination, but how do you get from here to there? There are no formulaic standard answers. You've been given the map and tools, and you have a sense of the different choices available to you. Living each moment with full presence will reveal the way forward. It unfolds step by step. Every individual, every relationship, and every team is going to experience a different version of the journey. This is the map; it is not the territory. Once you start walking it, you will discover many things.

Start by cultivating presence to get powered by Shakti. From there, work to build the capacities of wholeness, flexibility, and congruence. Become your own mother-father and your own beloved. Nurture and protect your inner child; love and set yourself free to come of age and play the game of life, the *lila*, joyfully and consciously. Find that family reunion within you, psychologically. Know how to switch between masculine and feminine energy and not get stuck in one or the other. Stay on purpose and live your dharma.

You are already en route to your fulfillment. Use your myth, your story, to journey joyously, without needless suffering and angst. Experience the equanimity that comes with knowing and accepting that the only way out is in and through. Everything begins from your inner self.

Not journeying is not an option. If the human race is to be saved and elevated, each of us needs to wake up, make the journey, and answer the call to adventure. There is, in Martin Luther King Jr.'s words, a "fierce urgency of now," a joyous, ecstatic urgency, the pull of what could be. It is not about evading the flames below but reaching for the fruit above.

Awakening for Planetary Change

Futurist Faith Popcorn has said: "The end of gender is not about societal androgyny. It is about the integration and emerging dominance of feminine energy. We are at the end of combative feminism, patriarchal dominance, and one-dimensional identity."[6]

At a subconscious level, many women are still prisoners of stereotypes, unmet expectations, and unconscious biases. They have great latent power that they fail to exercise. As Marti Barletta says, "Women have all the power that matters; they have buying power, wealth, and political power. But bizarrely, nobody seems to know that. It is time for us to be bolder. We have the critical mass: we're 51 percent of professionals and managers now, 53 percent of entry level into business executive ranks. It's time to stop trying to blend in. We tried to convince everybody that we were as much like the guys as possible, with our quarterback shoulder pads in the '80s. We need to help people understand that what we bring to the party is strong and smart and different from what men bring. Like everything in diversity, differences add to the mix."[7]

But is "leadership" in the sense of top positions the only path to change? Of course not, though we would all benefit from having many more women in leadership roles than we do today. Marti Barletta points out that "One of the key benefits for many men of being the top dog is that you're the top dog. Not as many women as men care that much about being top dog or are willing to sacrifice everything else in life to get the slot."[8] What this points to is that we need to change the way we think about leadership so that it becomes a more human undertaking—one that doesn't ask people to forgo other vitally essential things in life.

Women need to step up and step out, but not as pale imitations of men. They should confidently take hold of the reins of power to use that power in creative, life-affirming ways. Iconic singer and songwriter Alanis Morissette expresses it beautifully: "The definition of success for me is win-win or no deal, as Stephen Covey said. In my mind, it is the divine feminine at play. Whether it is multimillion-dollar business deals, or what park we're going to for my son, it's win-win or no deal. To me, that is success: if we can find a win-win, and we can walk away from something where there is no win-win."[9]

REVIVING WOMEN'S CIRCLES

We were not just put on this planet to be thinking creatures; we are also part of nature, just as much as the oceans and forests and all the creatures in them. We need to understand Shakti as the earth and as the spirits of the land and the forces of the elements—all are different aspects of the same Shakti. This force, this abundance, moves us and is all around us.

We need a special form to enter into relationship and communication with nonhuman elements. That form is ritual. The root of the word "ritual" is the Sanskrit *ritu*. It refers to tradition, rhythm, seasons, and the menses. Devising meaningful rituals and bringing them to the workplace is a distinctly feminine way of leading.

The women's circle is one such ritual. It is a way to get in touch with the archetypal energies inside us. It is a setting in which women can give voice to their deepest fears, hopes, needs, angst, and pain. We surface them from the dark, suppressed places where we have stored them away. We bring them up and offer them to the central fire so we can be emptied of them. When we can empty ourselves, we are then ready to receive a new, higher consciousness, a capacity and ability to know how to handle life's challenges. So a circle is a way to empty the cup in order to fill it again. These circles are like cauldrons, alchemical spaces for the healing of humanity.

When we do something in a group with the intention to heal and evolve—not just ourselves individually, but collectively—it takes on higher levels of amplification, and profound outcomes become possible.

Several kinds of circles can be used, such as healing circles, dialogue circles, trust circles, divine feminine circles, and yogini circles. The core process of circle work can also be used in the workplace to run effective, inclusive, and efficient meetings.

Here we share the process of Shakti circles, which can be used by women to understand and connect with Shakti. It is a synthesized ritual, drawing from ancient traditions such as the Native American talking-stick and the Indian *homa* or *yagna* fire ceremony, as well as modern processes devised by consciousness facilitators we have interacted with and learned from.[10]

The Shakti Circle

In a Shakti circle, we consciously work with the evolutionary force of Shakti itself. Shakti is in us and working through us, through our *chakras* (our yogic energy centers), seeking to get more and more conscious as our energy rises up. We invoke the *panchamahabhuta*, the five elements (earth, water, fire, air, ether/space) that are around us and inside us. Become aware of how those five elements come together in your creative womb; this is where the alchemy takes place.

Use a tree as a centering device and as a visual metaphor for your spine. It serves as a sacred access *mandala* (a geometric figure representing the universe in Hindu and Buddhist symbolism), which brings the supreme consciousness down to earth, and connects the consciousness of the earth with the source above. We invite every woman in the circle to feel her womb connect with the earth below and heaven above. Become the collective womb, not just for yourself but to cleanse and heal and transform whatever it is you carry as a woman in your body-mind. We are together not just to heal our own selves. We're healing womanhood, the accumulated pain and psychic wounds from thousands of years of patriarchy.

We invite everyone's intention to connect with that level of being—to speak from her Shakti, the core creative power from which they have emanated, the animating force of the conscious-ness principle. (Recall that in yoga we call the consciousness principle Shiva, the masculine, and we call its creative, dynamic, executive force and power Shakti.)

The circle has some important rules. Start by creating an al-tar of fire as the centerpiece for the circle. If you can't sit around a fire, try using a mandala of candles or tea lights and flowers. If possible, float the candles in an *urli*, a wide and flat water-filled vase that sits on the floor. Then invite the women to become quiet and sit in a circle around it. Always begin by invoking everyone's higher self for guidance and protection, and for the highest healing outcomes. Surrender the whole ritual to the di-vine Shakti.

Whenever you speak, speak your truth. Use a "truth-object," a touchstone. When it comes to you, hold it and speak from your heart, not from your mind. Tell it as it is; don't sugarcoat anything. Listen deeply to the content but equally to the *intent* when others speak. Allow yourself to be moved. You're trying to get in touch with the collective, the Shakti that's speaking through each per-son. If doubts and questions or judgments come up in your mind when someone else is speaking, stop and silently observe, "Hmm . . . how interesting that this person should feel this way." Let it be a wondering rather than a judgment. Allow for a spacious period of deep silence after each person speaks. Let the silence breathe. Absorb and digest what has just been spoken before speaking. Ground yourself, anchor yourself, and speak only when you feel centered. There's no compulsion to speak; pass the touchstone on to the next person if you have nothing to say. Do not interrupt or challenge another.

The most important thing is to elicit the unsaid. The whole point of the circle is to speak what has not been spoken. This is a safe and sacred space for you to release and let go that which you have held inside. Offer every word to the central fire, not to each other. Do not make eye contact; speak directly to the fire and let it go.

That which is deeply personal is completely universal. Whatever you say, however personal it may be, know that it's a completely universal truth, and it is part of many women's stories on this planet.

Every time the touchstone goes around the circle, the leader calls out one question. The question is offered to the fire and to the women in the circle. There are some very key and powerful transformative questions to connect with, release, heal, and transform Shakti. Feel free to speak as much as you need to but keep it as succinct as possible. As you offer your closing words, breathe up the whole intention behind them and offer it to the fire to feel truly cleansed of that material.

When the touchstone comes to you, answer the first question:

As a woman, what brings you joy?

Take a deep breath. Connect with your womb. Connect with the five elements inside you and all around you. Connect with the Shakti inside you, the creative power of the universe. Connect also with your own personality, your ego self, which has journeyed this far. Nilima might say, "As a woman, what brings me joy is my body. I feel deeply delighted that I have a beautiful, dancing body, and that this body has been so faithful. It's been such an amazing partner. It's been with me every step of the way and responds to my commands, my prayers, my intentions. I just want to give thanks to this beautiful body and for the fact that I can dance with it." As you hear every woman speak, feel her joy, connect with your own joy, and amplify the joy in the circle.

Other questions that are typically used:

What causes you pain/fear/anger/shame/guilt?

What do you need to love/accept/forgive/let go/fully grieve?

Sense your way into the circle's wisdom and allow new questions to emerge as you hear what comes up.

As this is a powerful, alchemical space, sensitive topics may surface. Be ready for conflicted psychological forces of resistance or obstruction getting stirred up—forces that could potentially derail the process. When it comes, see it for what it is with presence; invoke and apply your highest Shakti- and Shiva-like wisdom and compassion to contain it—or park it with humor and move on. Each circle becomes a mini heroic journey in itself, especially for the circle leader.

Restoring Gender Relations: Whole Man, Whole Woman, One Dance

In our work aimed at restoring gender relations, we also run "Whole Man – Whole Woman" circles. This is a process in which an equal number of men and women are invited to sit in concentric circles. First, the inner circle is run for women, while the men are asked to simply sit in the outer circle, hold the space, and bear silent witness, without judgment or resistance, to the voice of "everywoman" they hear as a set of collective, universal themes. Next, the places are exchanged: the women sit in the outer circle and the men voice their deepest hopes, fears, and needs. They answer the same questions, starting with the words, "As a man . . ."

Needless to say, what unfolds is poignant and deeply revelatory for each group about their own reality and that of the other. Men especially have not been socialized to truly feel their feelings and allow themselves to be vulnerable in a safe way. Both groups are usually shocked by the surfacing of the lesser known but extremely significant "masculine wound" around issues such as feelings of inadequacy in their fatherhood, their ability to provide for their loved ones, and their personal legacy.

A profound compassion, what Buddhists call *mahakaruna*, takes over the space, as each group is able to better understand and forgive themselves and each other. All take away a lasting sense of respect and acceptance of their interdependent existence.

TURNING OUR DRIVES INTO OUR POWER BASES

Just as the drama triangle can be made into a conscious dharma triangle, we can also make conscious the drives of the four-fold self and use them as power bases for our leadership. These drives are within us whether we acknowledge them or not. Together, eros, thanatos, logos, and mythos fuel our journey to individuation.

Sri Aurobindo, in his book *The Mother*, describes the four main powers of Shakti that together enable the conscious life. These are the qualities of harmony, strength, wisdom, and perfection. We are graced with these qualities when we offer up our ego self and replace it with authentic presence.[11]

FOUR-FOLD SELF	ARCHETYPES OF MATURE LEADERS	POWERS OF SHAKTI
• Logos	• Sovereign	• Wisdom
• Thanatos	• Warrior	• Strength
• Mythos	• Magician	• Perfection
• Eros	• Lover	• Harmony

Adapted from King, Warrior, Magician, Lover *by Robert Moore and Douglas Gillette, and* The Mother *by Sri Aurobindo.*

As a Shakti Leader, you are invited to cultivate presence and engage with and examine your inner drives. You may find that when you evoke eros, it yields a state of harmony and flow within. Thanatos offers up strength, logos bestows wisdom, and mythos brings you into a more complete perfection. Harmony and strength are eros-thanatos made conscious; similarly, logos-mythos reveals wisdom and perfection.

Furthermore, as you come into your own as an adult leader, you may well find yourself flexing between the four main archetypes of a mature psyche that Jungians offer: the Sovereign (King/Queen), Warrior, Magician, and Lover.[12] The Sovereign has mastered logos, the Warrior thanatos, the Lover eros, and the Magician mythos.

Consciously creating an approach to leadership that is your unique blend of the four bases of Shakti (harmony, strength, wisdom, perfection) will help you make your innate drives conscious and harness them to fuel you. Presence enables making your unconscious drives conscious. The four main aspects of Shakti offer bases of true power to draw upon, instead of being driven by ego-shadow power plays within and around you.

As you leverage the four main powers of Shakti, you may find them to be conscious presences within you—presences that you can access and manifest as needed. Much like your higher self, they too respond to prayer, invocation, and affirmation. Deep and fulfilling connections are safely possible with these Shakti-forces, which partner with us as long as we are in selfless service to our higher purpose and greater good.

Of these four leadership archetypes, one may be most resonant with your preferred way of being, your *swabhav*. You should anchor yourself in this power source while drawing from the other three as needed.

You are not doomed to be churned by your unconscious forever. You can make the innate drives of your ego-shadow self conscious and gain access through them to the power of your higher self.

A New Mythology for a New Consciousness

We need to evolve a new mythology if we are to reach for a new consciousness with a new understanding of power. We also need to re-tell some of the old myths from this new consciousness—myths that were interpreted by the old patriarchal consciousness of an immature humanity. Keeping outdated systems and ways of being in play simply does not serve us anymore. For example, Sita, the heroine of the ancient Indian epic the Ramayana, is exalted as the dutiful and chaste wife of Rama, who is an incarnation of the divine preserver Vishnu himself. Many women in India and around the world who relate to the myth are newly interpreting it and re-telling it from the point of view of an empowered Sita, mistress of her destiny. As they do so, they heal their own story and create a more appropriate and effective personal myth.

A New Mythology for Business

Joseph Campbell was a strong advocate for a new "mono-myth," which he felt was essential for humanity to survive. The Conscious Capitalism movement is seeking to create a new mythology for business—one in which business has a higher purpose beyond profit, conscious leaders who are mature and fully human, caring cultures built on love and trust, and win-win partnerships with all stakeholders.

This movement arrives at a time when the digital age has pushed the economy into a new phase. It is largely exemplified and led by young entrepreneurial minds and bodies, unburdened by the outdated myths of old business predicated on a view that is now widely recognized as selfish, instrumental, and narrow.[13] They thrive on the power of new ideas, and operate as creators who are reimagining the world instead of trying to incrementally change the existing baggage-ridden institutions that are either unable or unwilling to adapt to the times.

Before this new age of business gets conditioned into its own mythology (for everything eventually needs one to drive and sustain it), we offer "Embracing Feminine and Masculine Power in Business" for consideration. Evolution and history have tasked today's leaders, as creators of a new economy based on the power of ideas, with the daunting but joyous responsibility of reimagining a new world—*a world that works for all*. By actively embracing the idea of becoming more conscious by tapping into Shakti, today's leaders can show the way.

We must choose the new myth wisely, consciously embracing the pooled power of the feminine and the masculine to liberate the heroic spirit of business to elevate humanity. Everything else will fall in place after that: the vision, capacities, values, competencies, behaviors, and desired outcomes for leadership and for the enterprise.

IN CLOSING

The human inner experience of eros-thanatos and logos-mythos has long been a veritable battlefield, a *kurukshetra* of the war between the masculine and the feminine for supremacy over the other, tragically canceling/destroying each other in the bargain. They have been, in Jung's words, "opposites that come together in the conjunction . . . either confronting 'one another in enmity' or attracting 'one another in love.'"[14] Now that we have seemingly exhausted all ego/fear-based possibilities, we are ready to lay down our swords and bask in the infinite possibilities of soul-based love.

Understanding, acceptance, and forgiveness are needed all around. It is now time for the masculine and the feminine to partner with the other rather than seeking to dominate — like antigens and antibodies working with each other to bring about an indestructible resilience of our embodied being.

Shakti Leaders Speak: On Flying in Circles

Author and activist Lynne Twist offers a compelling metaphor to describe the metamorphosis that we are collectively experiencing:

Something that's happening right now in the world is what I call the Sophia Century—the century when women will take their rightful role in equal partnership with men. There's a wonderful prophecy from the Native American people called the prophecy of the eagle. It says that, for many centuries, the bird of humanity has been flying primarily with one wing, and that wing is the male wing. The female wing has not been fully extended; it's been held back and not been fully expressed, while the male wing, in order to keep the bird of humanity afloat, has gotten overdeveloped and has actually become violent, and the bird of humanity has been flying in circles as a result. This is the century when the female wing of humanity, or feminine expression, will fully extend itself. When it does so, the male wing will be able to relax and the bird of humanity will soar, rather than fly in circles. That metaphor is so moving, because it doesn't make men wrong. I feel that in myself; when I'm fully expressed in both the energy of the masculine and feminine parts of who I am, I soar. I soar as a leader; I soar as a follower; I soar as a human being. When I'm withheld or stymied or feel oppressed or weak as a woman and try to compensate by using my male energy too much, I fly in circles.[15]

It is perhaps India's spiritual destiny to harness and synthesize all the world's spiritually divergent forces. As author and scholar Neela Bhattacharya Saxena has said, "The contribution of Indian civilization to the world has been the technology that it developed for thousands of years: the science of interiority, how to go inside, how to really integrate. That is what yoga is. That technology has already come into the Western world. If we can connect the dots, there's no such thing as East-West anymore."[16]

With respect and in the spirit of service, we have offered the idea of Shakti here as a piece of profound yogic wisdom that has great potential to transform our world by helping all of humanity move forward with love and grace. For far too long, half of humanity has been trapped and kept subjugated. We have also disavowed half of our psyche, the part that renders us truly and deeply human, the aspect that is most closely connected with our higher selves and our divine natures.

Shakti Leadership knits all the diverse elements together into an intricate tapestry that extends beyond man-woman, straddles East and West, blends the indigenous and modern, as well as the human, archetypal, and divine. It includes everyone and subjugates no one. It seeks to create a world in which everyone flourishes and blossoms—a world in which we can all win.

Humanity is poised on a massive evolutionary tipping point, moving inexorably forward to its divine destiny of *ananda* or bliss. The chaos we are experiencing is not a breakdown but a breakthrough, a massive labor of the divine Shakti birthing a new consciousness. If we choose to see it as a clarion call to live joyously and evolve consciously to the life divine, we can welcome a new age of an awakened, thriving humanity.[17]

We believe that the ultimate objective of nature's evolution is to achieve a perfected humanity and planet, functioning as a single organism in harmony and balance. May women and men step in, step up, and step out together. Let Shakti take the lead and show the way for them to hold up the whole sky together!

Whole man, whole woman, whole world. Manifesting Shakti. May the Force (Shakti) be with you.

Let's dance!

Epilogue

SHAKTI SPEAKS

Shakti Speaks started in February 2014 as a monthly column by co-author Nilima Bhat, based on dialogues within the Women's Circle, an initiative by *DNA*, a national newspaper in India. The goal of the column is to restore gender relations and empower women to raise their consciousness and connect with the primordial power within.

A diverse group of women of different age groups and educational and working backgrounds came together in Shakti Circles to explore their deepest hopes, fears, and needs. They addressed questions such as: As a woman, what brings you joy? What causes you pain, fear, and anger? What do you need to love, accept, forgive, and let go?

What emerged—the range and depth of material uncovered and processed—surprised us all. The issues broadly fell into five themes: Motherhood, Vulnerability, Women vs. Women, Invisibility, and Longing. Each is an existential issue of deep significance.

Based on the psycho-spiritual nature of the themes, and Nilima's addressing of them from a yogini's perspective, these columns have developed as a modern-day "Gita for Women" where Shakti gives divine instruction to Sadhana on what her dharma should be. (Sadhana represents Everywoman. Her name means "self-mastery practice.")

Unlike the dialogue between Krishna and Arjuna (which is the basis for the revered Indian text the Bhagavad Gita), there is no such dharmic dialogue available from the Mother Goddess to Everywoman, who is her emanation, her child. So the column evolved into *Shakti Dialogues—Everywoman in Conversation with Her Eternal Self*. It is a healing, psycho-spiritual follow-up to Eve Ensler's acclaimed "Vagina Monologues" in the women's issues space.

REDEFINING MOTHERHOOD

Why does motherhood still define women? Why is a woman's life considered incomplete without experiencing motherhood? Why is it the be-all and end-all of a woman's existence?

Sadhana came home in tears. It was her tenth wedding anniversary, and she had worn her new sari, kissed her husband good morning, and left for work in happy anticipation of her promotion that was to be announced that day. She had worked hard for it and she certainly deserved it. Life was good.

Halfway through the day, her mother called. Sadhana proudly announced her new job title, expecting her mother to feel joy at her achievement. (Somewhere in the back of her mind, her mother's voice always egged her on, to shine and do better. She felt like an eight-year-old again who had come home with her report card saying "1st rank," her mother glowing with pride.)

"This is not a time to be proud, dear girl. I just had a call from your mother-in-law. What are you up to? It has been ten years and you still haven't conceived! What are you waiting for? The clock is ticking and you are running out of eggs. You were not a spring chicken when K married you. Enough of this career business. You've had your fill of meeting your personal ambitions, now get on with motherhood."

Sadhana put the phone down with trembling hands. The ghost had returned to haunt her again. K and she had not told the rest of the family about their several trips to the fertility clinic in the last four years. The series of "almost" pregnant moments and failed attempts had taken its toll on both of them, and they had finally decided that if it were to happen naturally, it would.

K had thrown himself back into his work and so had she. Yet, lately, women in the office seemed to be getting pregnant left, right, and center, flaunting their baby bumps. Something ever so small would stir in her that she would quickly repress before she could even feel it.

Her mother's call broke the camel's back on whatever it was she had kept such a tight lid on. As soon as she got home, she rushed to her altar and shuddered her way open to a tsunami of confused feelings, images, and unnamed forces that overcame her. She didn't really know why she was crying. Her tears were hers and yet, they felt as if they were coming from beyond her . . . as if she were suddenly bringing forth the pain of every woman who had not borne a child.

It was funny. She thought she had made peace with being childless and now she couldn't understand her own upheaval.

"Why does motherhood still define women?" she wailed. In this day and age where we stand shoulder to shoulder with men in education and the workplace, why is a woman's life still considered incomplete without experiencing motherhood? Why is it the be-all and end-all? "Am I not in charge of my own destiny, and my body? Do I not have a right to choose how I live my life? Can it not include motherhood?" Even as she said it, she felt that strange, vague unease somewhere in her womb. This time she decided not to ignore it.

Her breath slowed down and she became very still. Like some kind of Alice in Wonderland, she seemed to be drawn in through the vortex of her navel . . . back into a dark space, deep inside her womb . . . or was it her mother's womb? It just was A Great Dark Womb.

Suddenly, her angst, her pain, and her fear all seemed to dissolve. It was if she had entered a secret, sacred, eternal space.

It felt like home, but unlike any actual home she had ever lived in. Her whole being relaxed deeply into an indescribable feeling of comfort.

The Void was powerful and alive. She sensed a presence — one more real than herself. It seemed to be flowing through her every cell, even as she was bathed in it from all around. "Who are you?" Sadhana asked in awe.

The presence replied:

> I am Shakti. I am the Great Mother, the Creative Power, from whom this multiverse has come forth. From every planet, star, and galaxy to plants, animals, and humans. Even the angels, gods, and those you call demons.

> Like you, each is a unique aspect of all that I hold in my being. In an eternal, endless *lila* (play), I create and recreate myself in all the ways in which I can experience the *ananda* (bliss) that I AM.

> You came out of my womb so I can now come out through yours, in every way that you give life to what brings you joy, when you create beauty and expressions that vitalize and power the cycles of life.

> Up until now, life on your planet is propagated through the children you give birth to. Every time you give birth, you become divine, and in that you fulfill your greatest potential, your manifest divinity. You experience the power of giving life and its ineffable ecstasies.

> In the new age that is upon you now, my presence in your womb seeks to fulfill us all, expressing powers and mysteries of untold beauty and magnificence that will not just resolve the problems your species has created for itself, but evolve the planet and its consciousness to a whole new level. Your womb and your woman's body contain the seeds of capacities, gifts, and wisdom you will birth and bring forth into the world, whether or not you choose to birth a human child.

The world today is a transition from the old ways to the new. Don't fret for being caught in beliefs that don't serve you anymore. They will pass, to be replaced by values that are appropriate for the Conscious Life that is manifesting. As a woman, your womb is an exquisite resource that you will have to use to bring forth creative ideas and expressions for the new age. Take good care of it. Listen to its wisdom and rest in its regenerative powers. Become your own mother; give birth to and nurture your new child-self who will grow up and thrive with the ways of the awakened feminine.

You are tasked to now become a mother to the world, not to just one or two children. The "discomfort" you feel in your body every time you see pregnant women is just my presence that you are now pregnant with. I am glad you finally looked in. You are indeed pregnant—as is every man and woman at this time—with me. It is my consciousness that is breaking upon and awakening in the world at this time. Pay close attention and bring me forth in every way you can.

Every time you lay down your swords against each other as men and women and see each other equally as my children, you give birth to me. Every time you manifest works of high aesthetic form, come up with inclusive solutions to problems, let go with tough love all that doesn't serve you anymore, and embrace the dark side with compassion and wisdom, you give birth to me. You experience motherhood in a way that honors and fulfills your body's divine potential.

When you can define motherhood in this way, can you see that it is indeed the be-all and end-all of being a woman? Embrace this new reality for yourself, dear child, self of my own Self. Turn your problem on its head. Say yes to motherhood by becoming a mother to the world.

VULNERABILITY:
STRENGTH OR WEAKNESS?

Is there an appropriate level of displaying/being vulnerable?
As a woman, my concern is "My gentleness should not be
taken as a sign of my weakness." Our lachrymal (tear)
glands are often hyperactive. We cry when we are sad, angry,
happy, or while chopping onions! Barring the last one,
what is it with women and tears? Psychosomatic? Social
conditioning? Physiological evolution/regression? I get the
need to vent, the cathartic relief from crying. I don't get why
the tears are sometimes helpless.

"What is it with women and tears?!" Sadhana was sitting in front of her altar. Her face showed all her confused emotions — from sadness to anger to exasperation to just a plain unknowable *feeling*. For no reason at all she had burst into tears in her appraisal interview.

She had gone in super-confident. She had worked hard and had so much to show for it. She knew she was competing against two very logical, competent male colleagues, who seemed to know exactly where they stood in the scheme of things. They knew how to play the game, how to compete in the dog-eat-dog world. She too had learned the same skills very well. Long ago she had promised herself, "My gentleness will not be taken as my weakness." When she overheard her juniors snicker that she was a "man in woman's clothing," far from being affronted, she had been secretly pleased.

Then her HR head had asked, "You know you have to move to the Naxalite area as part of your promotion. Are you sure as a woman you are up to it?" (The Naxalite movement is a violent uprising in parts of eastern India.)

She had anticipated that question, rehearsed her carefully chosen blasé, brave words. Yet, suddenly, out of nowhere, her throat tightened, her voice thickened, her face crumpled and tears welled up . . .

Those god-awful tears!

"See, Sadhana, we hire people regardless of their gender. You are expected to do a job. All promotions here are based on that competence alone. Do not expect any mollycoddling or 'fair sex' treatment. Emotions have no place in a meritocracy."

Sadhana apologized as she hurriedly ended the interview and left the room. Even as she berated herself for her loss of composure, she knew she had somehow failed . . . not just the interview but herself.

And so here she was, at her altar, her refuge. Her gaze searched for strength in the eyes of her beloved deities and sacred objects given by her mother and collected from temple and church stalls. She had failed them all. She was so sorry to be just a weak, weepy woman after all.

"Mother, how do I stop *feeling*? It is feelings that make me vulnerable. They are my Achilles heel! No matter how hard I try to crush them, deny them, be strong and stoic, they just won't go away. If I repress them, I become numb and feel like an automaton, as if something in me is dead. When I suppress my fears, guilt, shame, I also can't feel joy, harmony, beauty, the *goodness* of life.

"I may stuff my feelings and learn to live rationally, but why can't I control tearing up? It is so embarrassing, humiliating, and disempowering when I just burst into tears at the most inappropriate times. I don't just cry when I am sad. I cry when I am angry or helpless and even when I am supposed to be happy! My vulnerability is my weakness. Its display is inappropriate! I get taken advantage of because of it."

And the all-seeing and compassionate Great Mother spoke:

My child, all is indeed well. It is just as I have intended. As a human and as a woman, you have a prime place in my Creation. You are here to unfold all the capacities of my own infinite nature. The feelings you are deploring, that make you vulnerable, are your most exquisite resource. Vulnerability is not a liability. It is an *ability* I have built into your system.

Your ability to be emotionally wounded is necessary for your complete, indestructible being to manifest all that it can be and all that it can experience.

Do you remember when you were a child and you fell sick with chickenpox? Your immune system got triggered to fight it and in the process your body developed a resilience and biological immunity to never catch that disease again. Feelings and emotions are my way of triggering your psychological immunity so you learn to bend, not break and become resilient like the bamboo.

But it is so much more than that! I haven't created you to simply survive. I have created you to thrive! To live fully and savor deeply every *rasa*, all the juice of life possible. This is my *lila*, my play. Through you I experience every possibility in *myself*.

The Age of Mind has overvalued rationality and reason, objectivity and an ascetic detachment as a sign of strength. When man denies his feelings and emotions as weaknesses, messy and unmanageable, he also denies my Shakti, the vitalizing power, the essence of vibrant life.

Your vulnerability is precious. Your wound keeps you real, in touch with all the creative potential awaiting you. It is not your weakness, it is your glory, your doorway to your true strength.

That's why I made feelings and emotions beyond the control of your thoughts and beliefs, which can limit you. Especially your tears! Those I wired directly to your body, which lives in the truth at all times. Your body cannot lie, and your tears cannot be controlled. You cannot fake them either. When my presence in your soul is touched, when you are touched by the truth of something, your raw, unconditioned, authentic core rejoices! For it knows it lives. It tells you it does by making the tears flow so you stop and take note! For a brief moment, the veil has lifted and my Mystery, the sacredness of life, is present in your slumbering, unconscious world of make-believe importance. Stop and enter through the doorway of your wound. On its other side lies your divinity, your indestructible vulnerability. Where you can claim your whole-woman, fully human self.

Rejoice and rest in the release of your wholeness! Even the gods envy your vulner-*ability*, for they do not feel the depths that you do.

WOMEN VS. WOMEN

Aren't women equally culpable in matters of patriarchy? Don't they practice favoritism at home against their daughters or daughters-in-law? I am always amazed why one woman (it could be the mother-in-law, boss, or sometimes even a colleague) can't understand another (sister, daughter-in-law, subordinate). The one who can give birth to male or female children, the one who is known for her forgiveness and her love—why does she lack understanding toward another woman? There are frequent power plays between women; why are we often our own worst enemies?

Sadhana switched off the TV in disgust. The program was a well-known scene from the Mahabharata, where Kunti tells her five sons to equally share Draupadi as a wife. Dutiful sons that they were, they did. No one asked what Draupadi had to say about that!

That part of the great story was not paid much attention to. Certainly not the way Sadhana had heard her own mother tell it. It was a footnote in a story about great warriors of dharma, Maharathis who fought the good fight.

A new consciousness was awakening in Sadhana these days; she found herself questioning things that in the past she had just accepted as normal. Suddenly there were unacceptable things everywhere she looked!

"Great Mother, Kunti had been a wife too. And an unwed mother. Surely she understood a woman's feelings and the sanctity of her body. She may have willingly borne great sons from different gods for the sake of their dynasty. But why did she assume Draupadi would—or worse, *should*—make that same choice? Or did women never have the power to choose anyway?

"But why berate our myths, which perhaps need to be reinterpreted for modern times? Look closer to home. Saroja, my *bai* who comes to clean our home and works in four other homes, is the main breadwinner of her family. Her husband is an alcoholic, and she has to drop off and pick up her young children from school, cook and clean and manage all chores, waking at 5:00 A.M. before everyone else and going to bed last. She has a mother-in-law and sister-in-law who live with them, who do not care to help her as it is considered her duty as the "good wife and daughter-in-law." Worse, they disapprove of her wearing jewelry or looking beautiful, as it may attract the attention of other men. All the saris I have given her are promptly taken by her mother-in-law to be given in dowry to the unmarried daughter. Saroja is not expected to have any desires of her own!

"Everywhere I look, I see this again and again, like a theater of the distorted. Are women not the empathic sex? Don't we feel love and kindness more than men? Why is it that we can shower it upon our fathers, husbands, and sons, but somehow we end up denying and discounting other women's voices and needs? Even when they are our own mothers, sisters, daughters, and colleagues?"

Shakti *speaks:*

> Always remember, my child, women are coming out of several thousand years of patriarchy, where the power has been in the hands of men. That power, arising out of my Shakti, is the fuel for all life.
>
> In their "dis-empowerment" from me, women have had to fight and feed on the scraps left over after the power play between men and the world they normed. Do not judge women too harshly, for they were caught in the same drama: the false belief that my Shakti is limited and to be traded as a weapon for survival.
>
> As both men and women have cycled through the use and abuse of power, the time has now indeed come for you to reinterpret your mythologies from a whole new level of consciousness.

I AM Shakti, the inexhaustible source-power of creation, preservation, and transformation, inside everyone. Awaken to me and rise out of *scarcity and fear* into *sufficiency and love.*

In your journey to reclaiming your power and becoming master of your own destiny, no one is your enemy, no one is your friend. All alike are your teachers.

Whether challenging you or supporting you, see the women in your life as together creating the perfect *kshetra* (field) for the distillation of your spirit, for the real you to shine through, resilient and inviolable! Together, they help you find and forge your dharma, your unique heroine's journey to becoming all that you can be!

See the truth of their being and give thanks, for they serve you in your evolution.

THE INVISIBILITY OF WOMEN

Three hundred years of the slave trade completely ravaged Africa. It created large tracts of desert. There were intertribal wars, hate, and paranoia. The slave traders' perspective was that black people were subhuman. Thinking that way absolved them from any sense of empathy with the victims. What has 5,000 years of subjugation and suppression done to women? How has it impacted our collective psyche? Women are still considered subhuman in many parts of the world. What is the implication?

Sadhana was deeply disturbed. She had just come home from attending her first women's circle. It was a gathering of women like she had never experienced before. Perfectly sane, "normal," educated, and emancipated women like herself had sat in a circle and shared their deepest hopes, fears, and needs. There was something about the circle and the process that had brought out truths that she had known but not been able to speak about. More disturbingly, truths she *did not even know she didn't know*—perhaps buried deep in her unconscious—had surfaced as

woman after woman shared. They surfaced truths about the in-
equity, inequality, negative stereotypes, and unconscious biases
that even women like her, educated and professional, still faced
in the twenty-first century!

Women in a "free society" still walk in fear of violation—
human beings who can be overpowered by others stronger
than them. In a day and age where we are questing for success
rather than survival, you would think our deepest fear would
be to fail. But Sadhana had heard again and again that every
woman's deepest fear is to be somehow *violated*—not just emotionally, but physically.

She mulled, "What has thousands of years of the patriarchy
done to our psyche?"

She had been called to the circle in a sudden urgency she felt
to find answers. There was something subhuman in the way a
group of men had physically overpowered and sexually abused
women in two horrific cases of rape in the major cities.

Sadhana trawled through the Internet in search of understanding and came across research on social dominance theory,
which studies how power tends to get polarized between dominant and subordinate social groups. There was an age of owners
versus slaves, then colonizers versus colonized, and, right through
it all, men versus women. When one social group dominated over
another, a strange psychological and behavioral phenomenon was
observed: the dominant group stopped "seeing" the subordinate
group. It was as if they became invisible to them. They were
subhuman, objects meant to serve the dominators' needs. The
subordinates were no different from the land or insentient materials to be mined or harvested or exploited.

Horrified as she started seeing the invisibility of women being
perpetrated in subtle and not-so-subtle ways in all domains of life,
Sadhana asked, "Mother? Why . . . ? How . . . ?"

A debilitating rage and shame rose up as she confronted her
own oft-experienced impotence and her invisibility.

In the great quiet of her being, Shakti speaks:

Come into your stillness, come to me. Let me breathe with you.

Being visible, being invisible.

Feeling comfort, feeling discomfort.

Breathe with me and master these polarities. Flow with each.

And find your freedom in that flow.

Be with one, then just as easily be with the other. Like inhale . . . and exhale.

Om Ma . . . Om Sri Ma.

Emergence now . . . Dissolution now.

Ease now . . . Churn now.

Allow each experience and move through each experience. With presence. And release me, your Shakti locked in them. Become. More. Power-full.

Look deeper. Is there perhaps a secret purpose to your humiliation? Humiliation leads to humility. In humiliation could lie the cradle of glory.

When you lose your sense of self-worth, your ego self experiences wounding. This pain and powerlessness cause you to journey within, awaken, and bring forth your true power, your Shakti. You then achieve your *real* worth, your worthiness to *be* and to *become* the all that is.

Exhale and disappear fully. Inhale and emerge truly.

Emerge to claim and fulfill your unique place in this grand evolution.

This is my built-in design, to evolve Creation.

It is okay to be visible. It is okay to be invisible. Both are choices for you to make and experience. Show up and shine through. Emerge out of the testing fire of your dominator. Equally, master invisibility and learn how to surrender your ego to my higher plan. *How else are you to come into your own, your true, enlightened power?*

LONGING

The unfair expectations that set us up and let us down.

"The minute I heard my first love story I started looking for you, not knowing how blind that was. Lovers don't finally meet somewhere. They're in each other all along."

Sadhana was stunned into a shocked silence as she read Rumi. The words of the thirteenth-century Persian poet and mystic seemed to speak to her with the freshness of a rose just bloomed.

She didn't completely grasp the full quote. Her breath was caught on just the first words: "the minute I heard my first love story I started looking for you..."

It seemed as if her breath had never moved away from that raw quest since.

Rumi knew her deepest secret?

She had been married ten years, and slowly it was dawning on her that she was still looking—despite having had a wonderful whirlwind romance with a kind, handsome man, a "prince charming" who married her and provided for her in every way.

Once the heady haze of the honeymoon period was over, she had suddenly felt a flat emptiness. No matter how hard she struggled to bring that "in love" feeling back, the cooking and housekeeping after the commute to work and back were pointing to a different kind of reality. The joke "after the ecstasy, the laundry" suddenly made sense and wasn't funny.

As K became a focused provider, holding down a steady job, managing the finances, and rising up the corporate ladder, Sadhana felt less and less seen and met as a desirable, charming woman. She had to find the romance she craved in mushy tele-serials or novels that absorbed her late into the night. Not to mention that it was also safer than having an affair!

These days it seemed as if she lived two lives: the one the world saw, where she was a dutiful, domesticated wife, and the secret life of her dreams where she went searching for an unnamed beloved, whose face she longed to see.

Not knowing what to do with this yearning that wouldn't go away, Sadhana came to her altar, her one refuge. "Mother, why can't I be happy? Despite having a faithful husband who provides so well for me. What is this longing? Why do I feel as if something precious is tantalizingly close but missing? Why do I feel like a desert waiting to be quenched by torrential rains?"

Shakti speaks:

Do not despair, my child. Your longing is my longing, for the ecstatic, life-giving union of body and spirit. I am your life-force seeking to dance with my lord inside you. He is Shiva, your awakened consciousness. When you merge with him, like a river finds the ocean, your thirst will be finally quenched. *Do not expect your husband or any man to fulfill you. That is the most unfair expectation and will only lead to certain disappointment.* Pay attention instead to the rest of Rumi's quote: "Lovers don't finally meet somewhere. They are in each other all along."

Wake up to Shiva. The Beloved we both seek is within. And he has loved you all along. He is the morning sun caressing your upturned face. The cool showers on your parched lips. The fragrant, warm earth after the first rains. The flowers blooming along your path in spring. The hot embrace of your husband on cold winter nights. Shiva makes love to you all year round. He has penetrated you so deeply, possessed you so completely. Don't you see?

Sleeping beauty, open your eyes and see the face of your beloved. He has been waiting for you to wake up and take you to pleasures beyond anything your innocence could conceive.

NOTES

Prologue

1. James Flynn, *Are We Getting Smarter? Rising IQ in the Twenty-First Century* (Cambridge, UK: Cambridge University Press, 2012).

2. Mirra Alfassa, *Rays of Light: Sayings of the Mother* (Pondicherry, India: Sri Aurobindo Ashram Publications Department, 1997), 169.

3. Martin Luther King Jr., "I Have a Dream" speech, delivered August 28, 1963, at the Lincoln Memorial, Washington, D.C., http://www .americanrhetoric.com/speeches/mlkihaveadream.htm (accessed December 2015).

4. Amy Adkins, "Majority of U.S. Employees Not Engaged Despite Gains in 2014," Gallup, January 28, 2015, http://www.gallup.com/ poll/181289/majority-employees-not-engaged-despite-gains-2014. aspx (accessed December 2015).

5. Mihaly Csikszentmihalyi, *Flow: The Psychology of Optimal Experience* (New York: Harper Perennial Modern Classics, 2008).

6. Chakras.net, "Shiva and Shakti," http://www.chakras.net/yoga-principles/22-shiva-and-shakti (accessed December 2015).

7. Swami Shankardev Saraswati and Jayne Stevenson, "What Is Shakti?" *Big Shakti*, August 19, 2015, https://www.bigshakti.com/ what-is-shakti/ (accessed December 2015).

8. Swami Nischalananda Saraswati, "Shiva & Shakti—The Twin Realities," *Yoga Magazine*, March 1991, http://www.yogamag.net/ archives/1991/bmar91/twins.shtml (accessed December 2015).

Chapter 1: Seeking Shakti

1. Sally Kempton, interview with Nilima Bhat and Raj Sisodia, March 16, 2015.

2. Lynne Twist and Teresa Barker, *The Soul of Money: Reclaiming the Wealth of Our Inner Resources* (New York: W.W. Norton & Co., 2006), 48–55.

3. Sally Kempton interview, op. cit.

4. Caryl Stern, interview with Nilima Bhat and Raj Sisodia, April 2, 2015.

5. Casey Sheahan, interview with Nilima Bhat and Raj Sisodia, April 1, 2015.

6. Jean Kilbourne, interview with Nilima Bhat and Raj Sisodia, April 1, 2015.

7. Ibid.

8. Ibid.

9. Ibid.

10. Jason Fonceca, "12 Top Feminine and 12 Top Masculine Traits That Could Change Your Life," Ryze Empire Design for Ambitious Creatives, January 31, 2012, http://ryzeonline.com/feminine-masculine-traits/ (accessed December 2015).

11. Ibid.

12. Sally Kempton interview, op. cit.

13. Colleen Barrett, interview with Nilima Bhat and Raj Sisodia, April 29, 2015.

14. Judy Sorum Brown, "Welcoming the Feminine Dimensions of Leadership," *Reflections: The SoL Journal* Vol. 4, No. 4 (2003): 49–54.

15. John Gerzema and Michael D'Antonio, *The Athena Doctrine: How Women (and the Men Who Think Like Them) Will Rule the Future* (San Francisco: John Wiley & Sons, 2013), 256.

16. Lynne Twist, interview with Nilima Bhat and Raj Sisodia, March 27, 2015.

17. Christopher Vogler, *The Writer's Journey* (Studio City, CA: Michael Wiese Productions, 2007). This is based on general principles of individuation (Jung) and other psychological schools such as Eric Berne's Transactional Analysis.

18. Vijay Bhat, unpublished work, June–September 2015.

Chapter 2: Leading with Shakti

1. Frank J. Williams, "The Women in Lincoln's Life," in *The Lincoln Forum: Rediscovering Abraham Lincoln*, ed. John Y. Simon and Harold Holzer (Bronx, NY: Fordham University Press, 2002), 25.

2. Leigh Buchanan, "Between Venus and Mars: 7 Traits of True Leaders," *Inc.* magazine, June 2013, http://www.inc.com/magazine/201306/leigh-buchanan/traits-of-true-leaders.html (accessed December 2015).

3. Lynne Twist, interview with Nilima Bhat and Raj Sisodia, March 27, 2015.

4. We would like to acknowledge the contributions of Vinit Taneja, Vijay Bhat, Arjun Shekhar, Gagan Adlakha, Arul Dev, and Kiran Gulrajani to the development of this unpublished model.

5. Judy Sorum Brown, "Welcoming the Feminine Dimensions of Leadership," *Reflections: The SoL Journal* Vol. 4, No. 4 (2003): 49–54. Used with permission of author.

6. Ron Shaich, panel discussion at Conscious Capitalism CEO Summit, Austin, TX, October 12, 2011.

7. Casey Sheahan, interview with Nilima Bhat and Raj Sisodia, April 1, 2015.

8. R. Edward Freeman, panel discussion at Conscious Capitalism CEO Summit, Austin, TX, October 12, 2011.

9. John Mackey, panel discussion at Conscious Capitalism CEO Summit, Austin, TX, October 12, 2011.

10. Fred Kofman, panel discussion at Conscious Capitalism CEO Summit, Austin, TX, October 12, 2011.

11. Ping Fu, interview with Nilima Bhat and Raj Sisodia, April 1, 2015.

Chapter 3: Presence: The Master Key

1. Joseph Campbell, *The Hero with a Thousand Faces* (London: Fontana, 1993), 44.

2. We would like to acknowledge the contributions of Vinit Taneja, Vijay Bhat, Arjun Shekhar, Gagan Adlakha, Arul Dev, and Kiran Gulrajani to the development of this unpublished model.

3. Jenna Goudreau, "Do You Have 'Executive Presence'?" *Forbes On-line*, October 29, 2012, http://www.forbes.com/sites/jennagoudreau/2012/10/29/do-you-have-executive-presence/ (accessed December 2015).

4. The Enneagram is a personality-typing framework with nine types of personalities. When we lose presence, three personality types of the nine tend to go to the gut and get in a defensive mode. Three personality types go to the heart and get into the mode of self-promotion. The last three personality types go to the head, and get into fear. See https://www.enneagraminstitute.com/ for more details.

5. Caryl Stern, interview with Nilima Bhat and Raj Sisodia, April 2, 2015.

Chapter 4: The Heroic Journey

1. Joseph Campbell, *The Hero with a Thousand Faces* (London: Fontana, 1993), 219.

2. Sally Kempton, interview with Nilima Bhat and Raj Sisodia, March 16, 2015.

3. Steve McIntosh, *Evolution's Purpose: An Integral Interpretation of the Scientific Story of Our Origins* (New York: SelectBooks, 2012).

4. Campbell, *The Hero with a Thousand Faces*, back cover.

5. Maureen Murdock, *The Heroine's Journey* (Boston: Shambhala Publications, 1990), 2, 187.

6. Ibid.

7. Clarissa Pinkola Estés, *Women Who Run with the Wolves: Myths and Stories of the Wild Woman Archetype* (New York: Ballantine Books, 1997); Sylvia Brinton Perera, *Descent to the Goddess: A Way of Initiation for Women* (Toronto: Inner City Books, 1981).

8. Murdock, op. cit.

9. Penelope Lively, introduction to *The Mythical Quest: In Search of Adventure, Romance & Enlightenment*, by Rosalind Kerven (Portland, OR: Pomegranate, 1996), vii–ix.

10. Jason Fonceca, "12 Top Feminine and 12 Top Masculine Traits That Could Change Your Life," Ryze Empire Design for Ambitious Cre-

atives, January 31, 2012, http://ryzeonline.com/feminine-masculine-traits/ (accessed December 2015).

11. Adapted from Murdock, op. cit., 5.

12. Ibid., 48–60.

13. Ibid., 48.

14. Men, on the other hand, tend to return to their original tribe and go on to transform it.

15. Sally Kempton, *Awakening Shakti: The Transformative Power of the Goddesses of Yoga* (Boulder, CO: Sounds True, 2013), 221–235.

16. Pinkola Estés, *Women Who Run with the Wolves*, 394–397.

17. Bruce Lipton, "Imaginal Cells in the Dying Caterpillar," YouTube video, https://www.youtube.com/watch?v=7DLokOQZlag (accessed December 2015).

Chapter 5: Becoming Whole

1. Casey Sheahan, interview with Nilima Bhat and Raj Sisodia, April 1, 2015.

2. Center for Integral Wisdom call, August 11, 2015, archived at http://www.ievolve.org/.

3. This material is adapted from Vijay Bhat and Nilima Bhat, *My Cancer Is Me: The Journey from Illness to Wholeness* (New Delhi: Hay House, 2013), 41–43. Adapted with the permission of Hay House Publishers India, New Delhi.

4. Michael Gelb presentation at Bentley University Conscious Capitalism Conference, May 17–18, 2011.

5. C. G. Jung, *Collected Works, Vol. 9, Part II* (Princeton, NJ: Princeton University Press, 1959).

6. This is a distillation of Carl Jung's teachings.

7. Maureen Murdock, *The Heroine's Journey* (Boston: Shambhala Publications, 1990), 4.

8. Ibid., 160

9. Murdock, *The Heroine's Journey*, 161.

10. Bhat and Bhat, *My Cancer Is Me*, 86–87. The following is extracted from *My Cancer Is Me*, "The Wounded Inner Child," as we believe this material maps onto the Shakti leadership journey in its entirety. Extracted with the permission of Hay House Publishers India, New Delhi.

11. Brian Skea, "Jung, Spielrein, and Nash: Three Beautiful Minds Confronting the Impulse to Love or to Destroy in the Creative Process," in *Terror, Violence and the Impulse to Destroy: Perspectives from Analytical Psychology*, ed. John Beebe (Einsiedeln: Daimon, 2003) (Kindle Location 5744-5973).

12. John Beebe, ed., *Terror, Violence, and the Impulse to Destroy: Perspectives from Analytical Psychology* (Einsiedeln: Daimon, 2003).

Chapter 6: Cultivating Flexibility

1. Presentation at Bentley University Conscious Capitalism conference, May 18, 2011, inspired by Rosabeth Moss Kanter.

2. Polarity mapping is described in detail in Barry Johnson, *Polarity Management: Identifying and Managing Unsolvable Problems* (Amherst, MA: HRD Press, Inc.). http://www.polaritypartnerships.com (accessed December 2015).

3. Lynne Twist, interview with Nilima Bhat and Raj Sisodia, March 27, 2015.

4. Mabel Collins, *Light on the Path* (London: George Redway, 1888). Adapted from original quote: "Intelligence is impartial; no man is your enemy; no man is your friend. All alike are your teachers."

5. Stephen B. Karpman, "Fairy Tales and Script Drama Analysis," *Transactional Analysis Bulletin*, 7.26 (1968): 39–43.

6. Betty Ann Heggie, "Making the Most of Your Energy Archetype," lecture, WIN Conference, Berlin, Germany, October 1, 2014.

7. Sally Kempton, interview with Nilima Bhat and Raj Sisodia, March 16, 2015.

8. Betty Ann Heggie, "Making the Most of Your Energy Archetype," lecture, WIN Conference, Berlin, Germany, October 1, 2014.

9. Adapted from Caroline Turner, "A Balance of Both Masculine and Feminine Strengths: The Bottom-Line Benefit," *Forbes*, May 7, 2012, http://www.forbes.com/sites/womensmedia/2012/05/07/a-balance-of-both-masculine-and-feminine-strengths-the-bottom-line-benefit/ (accessed December 2015). See also Caroline Turner, *Difference Works: Improving Retention, Productivity and Profitability through Inclusion* (Austin, TX: Live Oak Book Company, 2012) and http://www.difference-works.com (accessed December 2015).

10. Avivah Wittenberg, "The Company of the Future," lecture, WIN Conference, Berlin, Germany, October 2, 2014.

11. The four stages of competence learning model was developed by Noel Burch at Gordon Training International, http://www.gordon-training.com/free-workplace-articles/learning-a-new-skill-is-easier-said-than-done/ (accessed December 2015).

12. Cindy Wigglesworth, *SQ21: The Twenty-One Skills of Spiritual Intelligence* (New York: SelectBooks, 2012).

13. Eva Selhub, *The Love Response: Your Prescription to Turn Off Fear, Anger, and Anxiety to Achieve Vibrant Health and Transform Your Life* (New York: Ballantine Books, 2009).

Chapter 7: Achieving Congruence

1. Leigh Buchanan, "Between Venus and Mars: 7 Traits of True Leaders." *Inc.* magazine, June 13, 2013, http://www.inc.com/magazine/201306/leigh-buchanan/traits-of-true-leaders.html (accessed December 2015).

2. Casey Sheahan, interview with Nilima Bhat and Raj Sisodia, April 1, 2015.

3. From video shown by Joanna Barsh at Bentley University Conscious Capitalism conference, May 17–18, 2011.

4. Don Richard Riso and Russ Hudson, *The Wisdom of the Enneagram: The Complete Guide to Psychological and Spiritual Growth for the Nine Personality Types* (New York: Bantam, 1999), 48.

5. Debashis Chatterjee, paper in progress.

6. Casey Sheahan interview, op. cit.

7. Ibid.

Chapter 8: The Promise of Shakti Leadership

1. Sally Kempton, *Awakening Shakti: The Transformative Power of the Goddesses of Yoga* (Boulder, CO: Sounds True, 2013), 1.

2. From video shown by Joanna Barsh at Bentley University Conscious Capitalism conference, May 17, 2011.

3. Evidence of these is well summarize in Arianna Huffington's book *Thrive: The Third Metric to Redefining Success and Creating a Life of Well-Being, Wisdom, and Wonder* (New York: Harmony Books, 2014).

4. Chris Maddox, "The School of Nature," *The Wild Women Project Blog*, July 22, 2015, http://thewildwomanproject.com/2015/07/the-school-of-nature-wild-woman-initiation-lesson-1/ (accessed December 2015).

5. Caroline Myss post on Facebook, https://www.facebook.com/201192805715/photos/a.230879760715.284307.201192805715/10154475822725716/ (accessed December 2015).

6. Faith Popcorn at Bentley University Conference on Conscious Capitalism, May 17, 2011.

7. Marti Barletta, interview with Nilima Bhat and Raj Sisodia, May 28, 2015.

8. Ibid.

9. Alanis Morissette onstage interview at Success 3.0 Summit, Boulder, Colorado, October 31, 2014.

10. Including "The Tao of Facilitation" by Kiran Gulrajani and a women's circle by Valerie Gremillion.

11. The Mother (Mirra Alfassa), http://www.auro-ebooks.com/the-mother/ (accessed December 2015).

12. Robert Moore and Douglas Gillette, *King, Warrior, Magician, Lover: Rediscovering the Archetypes of the Mature Masculine* (New York: HarperOne, 1991).

13. John Kay, "Good Business," *Prospect Magazine*, March 1998.

14. C. G. Jung, "Mysterium Coniunctionis," *Collected Works*, Vol. 14 (Princeton, NJ: Princeton University Press, 1955/1963).

15. Lynne Twist, interview with Nilima Bhat and Raj Sisodia, March 27, 2015.

16. Neela Saxena, interview by Nilima Bhat and Raj Sisodia, April 3, 2015.

17. Kumar S. Sharma, *The Age of Ananda: Conscious Evolution to the Life Divine* (Los Angeles: Para Vidya Publishing, 2011), 192.

ACKNOWLEDGMENTS

This book has pretty much birthed itself, through an amazing series of synchronicities. Our book proposal to Berrett-Koehler would have passed as silently as another ship-in-the-night had Neal Maillet not been in the audience of Nilima's workshop (on Presence) at the Conscious Capitalism Conference organized by Raj at Bentley University in Boston some years ago. Neal was looking for compelling new ideas in the leadership space and was sufficiently impressed then to now want to hear what we had to say. Before we knew it, we had a contract for a book with "Shakti" as the main theme. Neal has been a warm and supportive presence in our lives ever since as our editor, and we are immensely grateful to him.

From then on to the authors' day arranged for us, we have been deeply impressed by Berrett-Koehler and their vision as well as their work ethic and culture. This is a high-purpose, conscious organization that truly lives its credo of "creating a world that works for all." We especially wish to thank founder Steven Piersanti, Jeevan Sivasubramaniam, Kristen Frantz, Katie Sheehan, and their colleagues at Berrett-Koehler. We would also like to thank our reviewers for their insightful and helpful comments and suggestions: Julie Clayton, Claire Pershan, Gauri Reyes, Kirsten Sandberg, and Anita Simha.

Vijay Bhat has been instrumental in countless ways to the conceptualization and development of this book, as Nilima's life and work partner for many years. Vijay is an incisive and strategic thinker, an inspiring and engaging teacher, a trusted advisor and a talented writer. We are deeply grateful for all his help and support.

We are deeply indebted to the many wonderful leaders and thinkers who shared their insights and stories in interviews. These include Marti Barletta, Colleen Barrett, Kristin Engvig, Ping Fu, Samit Ghosh, Sally Kempton, Jean Kilbourne, Frederique Apffel-Marglin, Neela Bhattacharya Saxena, Casey Sheahan, Caryl Stern, and Lynne Twist.

We would like to thank Sam Yau and the Esalen Institute for hosting two of our Conscious Leadership workshops, where many of these ideas were tested with the workshop participants. Esalen was also the site for several "Conscious Business Conclaves," where we deepened our understanding of conscious leadership.

We are grateful to Shubhro Sen for inviting us to lead a Shakti Leadership workshop at the hallowed Tata Management Training Center in Pune, India, and arranging for the videography; to Sanchi Illuri in Bangalore for her great job at painstakingly transcribing and pulling together the core material that would become the first cut of the manuscript; and, at the end, to Nic Albert in San Francisco, for his indispensable role in shaping and sharpening the manuscript and meeting our deadline even as he had to make a speedy recovery from pneumonia! We also thank Raj's graduate assistant at Babson College, Molly Quaid, for her outstanding research support at various stages of the book's journey. Raj would also like to thank his daughters, Priya and Maya Sisodia, for their extensive help in transcribing interviews and editing various drafts.

Permit us to add some personal notes here.

From Nilima:

"Finally, and perhaps above all, I acknowledge my esteemed co-author Raj Sisodia. Without him this book would simply not have been possible. He has been the kind of formidable partner most dream of but rarely find. Thank you, Raj, for your total faith in me and the message of this book, and for your generosity in making your academic scholarship and networks available for getting it out to the larger world."

From Raj:

"Working with Nilima on this project has been an extraordinary privilege. She is a cherished friend and life-changing teacher: a truly rare blend of penetrating intellect, voraciously wide learning, authentic presence, spiritual embodiment, and caring heart. This experience has opened my mind, heart, and spirit to countless new insights and possibilities."

INDEX

Italic numbers indicate figures or tables.

ABOUT THE AUTHORS

Nilima Bhat is a facilitator of personal transformation, coaching individuals and organizations in their quest for conscious evolution. She is an international speaker and trainer in organizational culture, conscious business, women in leadership, and self-awareness for work-life balance, as well as Indian wisdom and wellness traditions.

Previously, Nilima spent ten years heading corporate communications and public relations for major corporations such as ITC-Welcomgroup, Philips India, and ESPN STAR Sports.

Nilima graduated from St. Xavier's College, Mumbai, in life sciences and biochemistry, followed by a diploma in social communications media from Sophia Polytechnic, Mumbai. She later qualified as a yoga teacher from the International Sivananda Yoga Vedanta Centre and is a teacher-practitioner of the Integral Yoga of Sri Aurobindo and the Mother.

A trained dancer and choreographer, she has cofounded a professional dance company (Sri Shakti) whose mission is to demystify Indian dance and spiritual sciences for international audiences. Having lived and worked for ten years overseas (Singapore, London, Hong Kong), Nilima returned to India in 2004 with her husband to set up a leadership consulting firm, Roots & Wings, and an integrative medicine practice, Sampurnah. They are recently published authors of *My Cancer Is Me*, outlining their holistic and integrative approach to cancer.

A corporate refugee turned yogini, Nilima is now a global missionary. She travels the world leveraging her corporate experience and seventeen years of consciousness-based health and growth practices to help build enduring institutions and change-agents, especially women, who can lead the planet to sustainable solutions and positive impact. Her mission is the same as that of our publisher Berrett-Koehler: Creating a world that works for all. She also writes a column titled *Shakti Speaks*, initiated by a leading Indian media house, aimed at restoring gender relations and based on dialogues within women's circles.

Her integral approach synthesizes best practices and paths from around the world, and is customized to meet audience needs. Her particular expertise is in developing Body Intelligence and Spiritual Intelligence (BQ and SQ).

Nilima has delivered leadership training and facilitation for Microsoft, Whole Foods Market, Tata, Societe Generale Bank, Vodafone, and YPO, as well as academic institutions and developmental organizations such as Indus International School and SKS Microfinance. She is an active supporter of the Conscious Capitalism movement and Women's International Networking (WIN).

Approaching 50 and having "heroically journeyed" many times, through her mother's cancer, father's near-fatal car accident and brain injury, husband's cancer, and her own search for meaning from a sudden sense of failure in a thriving corporate career, Nilima looks back with amazement at her bucket list of world destinations that has very few places left to tick off. An avid traveler, Nilima has recently found great meaning in leading or joining Peace Pilgrimages to the world's sacred spots, from Kailash and Mansarovar in the Himalayas to Machu Picchu and Titicaca in the Andes. Comfortable in every culture and socioeconomic setting, from cleaning toilets to dining with CEOs and interviewing world leaders, Nilima speaks five languages and truly calls the whole planet "home."

Raj Sisodia is a globally recognized business academic who has done pioneering work in marketing and business strategy, marketing ethics and productivity, stakeholder management, and leadership. He is the FW Olin Distinguished Professor of Global Business and Whole Foods Market Research Scholar in Conscious Capitalism at Babson College. He is also co-founder and co-chairman of Conscious Capitalism Inc. He was previously Trustee Professor of Marketing and the founding director of the Center for Marketing Technology at Bentley University. He has an MBA from the Bajaj Institute of Management Studies in Mumbai, and a PhD in marketing from Columbia University.

In 2003, he was cited as one of "50 Leading Marketing Thinkers" and named to the "Guru Gallery" by the UK-based Chartered Institute of Marketing (the largest marketing association in the world). In 2007, he was honored with the "Award for Excellence in Scholarship" by Bentley University. In 2008, he received the "Bentley University Innovation in Teaching" award. He was chosen as one of twelve "Outstanding Trailblazers of 2010" by Good Business International, and one of 2010's "Top 100 Thought Leaders in Trustworthy Business Behavior" by Trust Across America. The author of eight books and more than 100 academic articles, Raj is best known as the lead author of *Firms of Endearment: How World Class Companies Profit from Passion and Purpose*. This book chronicled the unique, caring, and conscious attributes of 28 firms, showing how they deliver extraordinary value in multiple ways: high shareholder returns, thriving communities, customer well-being, and bringing a sense of meaning and purpose to the lives of their employees.

Raj is a leading figure in the fast-growing Conscious Capitalism movement and is on the board of trustees of Conscious Capitalism Inc. His book *Conscious Capitalism: Liberating the Heroic Spirit of Business*, co-authored with John Mackey, has made it to the *New York Times* and *Wall Street Journal* bestseller lists. His most recent book is *Everybody Matters: The Extraordinary Power of Caring for Your People Like Family* (with Bob Chapman). Raj has made more than 750 presentations at leading universities, corporations, nonprofits, and other organizations around the world. He has consulted with and taught executive programs for numerous companies, including AT&T, Nokia, LG, DPDHL, POSCO, Kraft Foods, Whole Foods Market, Tata, Siemens, Sprint, Volvo, IBM, Walmart, Rabobank, McDonalds, and Southern California Edison. He is on the board of directors at The Container Store.

Berrett–Koehler
BK Publishers

Berrett-Koehler is an independent publisher dedicated to an ambitious mission: *connecting people and ideas to create a world that works for all.*

We believe that to truly create a better world, action is needed at all levels—individual, organizational, and societal. At the individual level, our publications help people align their lives with their values and with their aspirations for a better world. At the organizational level, our publications promote progressive leadership and management practices, socially responsible approaches to business, and humane and effective organizations. At the societal level, our publications advance social and economic justice, shared prosperity, sustainability, and new solutions to national and global issues.

A major theme of our publications is "Opening Up New Space." Berrett-Koehler titles challenge conventional thinking, introduce new ideas, and foster positive change. Their common quest is changing the underlying beliefs, mindsets, institutions, and structures that keep generating the same cycles of problems, no matter who our leaders are or what improvement programs we adopt.

We strive to practice what we preach—to operate our publishing company in line with the ideas in our books. At the core of our approach is stewardship, which we define as a deep sense of responsibility to administer the company for the benefit of all of our "stakeholder" groups: authors, customers, employees, investors, service providers, and the communities and environment around us.

We are grateful to the thousands of readers, authors, and other friends of the company who consider themselves to be part of the "BK Community." We hope that you, too, will join us in our mission.

A BK Business Book

This book is part of our BK Business series. BK Business titles pioneer new and progressive leadership and management practices in all types of public, private, and nonprofit organizations. They promote socially responsible approaches to business, innovative organizational change methods, and more humane and effective organizations.

Berrett–Koehler
Publishers

Connecting people and ideas
to create a world that works for all

Dear Reader,

Thank you for picking up this book and joining our worldwide community of Berrett-Koehler readers. We share ideas that bring positive change into people's lives, organizations, and society.

To welcome you, we'd like to offer you a free e-book. You can pick from among twelve of our bestselling books by entering the promotional code **BKP92E** here: http://www.bkconnection.com/welcome.

When you claim your free e-book, we'll also send you a copy of our e-newsletter, the *BK Communiqué*. Although you're free to unsubscribe, there are many benefits to sticking around. In every issue of our newsletter you'll find

- A free e-book
- Tips from famous authors
- Discounts on spotlight titles
- Hilarious insider publishing news
- A chance to win a prize for answering a riddle

Best of all, our readers tell us, "Your newsletter is the only one I actually read." So claim your gift today, and please stay in touch!

Sincerely,

Charlotte Ashlock
Steward of the BK Website

Questions? Comments? Contact me at bkcommunity@bkpub.com.